LENNY BRUCE:
The Making
of a
Prophet

LENNY BRUCE:
The Making
of a
Prophet

a memoir by
William Karl Thomas

MEDIA MAESTRO - BOOK DIVISION

Cover design by William Karl Thomas
Copyright © 1989 by William Karl Thomas

ISBN 978-1-62768-003-5

Printed in the United States of America

This book is a memoir based on the best available information with the attempt to be as accurate and objective as possible. Any errors or omissions are purely accidental and unintentional. All of the photos were taken by the author, with the exception of one portrait of Frank Ray Perelli and six film production stills in which the author appears and which were taken with the author's camera.

Second English Edition Published October 2013

❖

MEDIA MAESTRO - BOOK DIVISION
P.O. Box 50672, Tucson AZ 85703
(520) 303-7805
info@mediamaestro.net
www.mediamaestro.net/books.htm

DEDICATION

This book is dedicated with
love and admiration to
Sally Marr
and
Frank Ray Perelli
without whom the world
would never have known of
Lenny Bruce.

Table of Contents

Chapter 1
IN THE BEGINNING

Six years before I started working with Lenny Bruce, I began my media career in the show-biz nightlife milieu of New Orleans's French Quarter, circa 1950. I had come from a small Gulf Coast town East of New Orleans that Tennessee Williams had lived in and written about. I didn't realize then that I had already lived some of the lives of Tennessee Williams's characters *(Sweet Bird of Youth, The Rose Tattoo,* and *This House Is Condemned* which I later worked on when it was filmed in that same little town), and that in the French Quarter I would live out still more of his characterizations.

I was working as a cocktail pianist only because I was eighteen and the Korean War made me eligible for the draft. Because I might be drafted at any time, I was unemployable except at such 'unsavory' jobs as the French Quarter nightclub district offered. Among my many misadventures there, which I now refer to as "my flaming youth," I began working for Shecky Greene and Frankie Ray, who owned a little after-hours club called The Wit's End. Their regular pianist, a fascinating and talented Englishman whose looks and humor were a carbon copy of Robert Benchley, would periodically get smashed and start depressing the customers with stories of the blitz in London where he lost his family. I ultimately inherited his job.

I was the youngest of a circle of regular entertainers there including Louie Prima, Fats Pechon, the Dukes of Dixieland, Pete Fountain, Al Hirt, and a Houdini-like character named Johnny Aladdin with whom I was later to write. The group included such leading strippers of the day as Stormy, Kalantan, and Lili Christine the Cat Girl.

Frankie Ray was ten years older than I and sort of took me under his wing. He appreciated what he called my 'touch of class,' an aura born of my 'genteel poor' (once wealthy but now destitute) origins and strengthened by the clientele of the club I originally worked in, gentry drifting in from the operas and concerts at Municipal Auditorium a few blocks away to hear me stumble through semi-classics with the saving graces of style and schmaltz.

Frankie was fascinated by my combination of knowledge and naivete. He delighted in seeing me distinguish between the dinner fork, the salad fork, and the fish fork; the soup spoon, the teaspoon, and the fruit spoon; the water glass and the finger bowl; yet openly salivate over the gourmet cuisine I never experienced in my childhood poverty. He was entertained by watching me unconsciously yet instinctively woo the clientele with my music, manners, and vocabulary, yet not even realize when a lady was making an overt pass at me by stuffing a twenty dollar bill in the kitty on the piano. Once he bent double with laughter when it was a fifty dollar bill and I ran two blocks trying to return her money, thinking she had made a mistake.

But what drew Frankie closest to me was that I remained naive enough to be a dreamer, and Frankie, too, was a dreamer at heart: dreams of success, of making it big, dreams of Hollywood. Frankie still worked on stage as the comedy emcee at Stormy's Casino Royal, and, every time the phone would ring behind the bar, he'd stop whatever he was doing on stage and ask, "Is that Hollywood calling?"

Of course, Hollywood never called. I saw practically all the comedy greats of the day pass through New Orleans and banter with Frankie, shooting one-liners at each other like it was a competition. They would buy a joke from him, or talk about the last time they worked together, while we'd munch on soft-shelled crab at Galatoire's, or lasagna at Domino's, or crayfish bisque at Brennan's. I saw Frankie pick up many a tab for movie stars in town to do a picture, with Frankie always in the bit part as the gangster, the Greek sailor, or the dope pusher. We got to know Mike Mazurki and all the 'bad guys' well, but somehow all the 'good guys' never picked up a check and never called from Hollywood to pay back a loan or return a favor.

In 1953 Korea finally caught up with me and I gambled on four presumably safer years in the Air Force instead of being drafted into two years of front-line infantry fighting a war I felt was an economic and political sham, a personal fight between President Truman and his rising competitor for the office, General MacArthur. The local columnists bid me a fond farewell, saying how nice I looked in blue, the ladies paid me many wistful and passionate goodbyes normally accorded a kamikaze pilot about to die, and then everyone promptly forgot me. Except Frankie.

I lost the gamble and, shortly after committing myself to four years in the Air Force, I found myself three miles from the front lines in Korea getting strafed at sunrise and bombed at sunset for a year. I never got hit, although one night a fuel dump at Inchon blew up while I was on guard, and when I looked up at the burning orange night sky it began to rain hot cinders that almost took out my right eye.

My greatest conflict was that I was in military Intelligence and obliged to evaluate reconnaissance photos which I knew might result in the people or objects under my scrutiny being annihilated. I would sometimes look down at a pair of stereo photographs showing human beings boarding camouflaged planes, and would think that those people probably just wanted to go home like I did, and if I failed to observe them in these photographs, their

3

chances might increase. Just about then some fifty-caliber slugs would rip through our tent or I would hear of someone I knew being shot dead, I would consider if any of the human beings in the photographs before me might have pulled the trigger, and I would complete my intelligence report with meticulous accuracy.

Frankie wrote me several times telling me how he and Shecky had bought the club I'd originally worked in so they'd have larger quarters for Wit's End. His handwriting was atrocious and his span of attention never survived more than a page, but his anecdotes and the girlie pictures he'd stuff in the letters to illustrate the adventures of our mutual friends sustained me and many of my fellow servicemen through a bitter and depressing winter. They were delighted to hear that Alouette had opened a tassel twirling school, that Evangeline the Oyster Girl had sold the huge oyster shell prop she would emerge from and married the boss, and that the Living Mermaid had her glass tank busted on stage by a jealous boyfriend with a fire ax and flooded 300 tourists out of Casino Royal.

Frankie had been chaperoning Lee Sharon for a while, a dancer of some success who was going with a mutual friend. Frankie used to park her in my club for me to guard while he worked, and I became enamored of her, plying her with keyboard renditions of *My Silent Love* while remaining fiercely loyal to my friendship with Frankie. When Frankie's letters told me she was unattached, I began to correspond with Lee from Korea. She said she was playing the Latin Quarter in Tokyo and I did all kinds of political handstands to get myself there, only to discover she had left three days previously. But the letters and even the hope of seeing her helped me then, and, like Frankie's letters and friendship and the dreams we shared together, began to give me an understanding of the importance and value of hope.

The night I arrived back in New Orleans after

4

returning from Korea, a cab screeched up to the curb where I stood on Bourbon Street, the door opened, and Frankie grabbed me by the collar dragging me into the cab like in a gangster movie. "You're just the man I need. We're going to play a benefit at an orphanage. So, all right, it ain't an orphanage, it's a reform school, so what the hell."

No hello, goodbye, I've missed you, or kiss my ass. "Why do you need me, Frankie? I'm sure a bunch of juvenile delinquents are gonna love hearing me play *Stardust* and *Tenderly*."

"Nothing to it, kid." I was always the kid. "Just play me on and off with a vamp, you know, ta-ta-ta-ta-tada, and when I tell them you're just back from Korea, they'll give you more applause than me."

He did, and they did.

On the way back to Felix's Restaurant I gave him an elaborately engraved sterling silver pocketknife I had carefully selected for him in Japan because it had manicuring accessories. He looked horrified and tossed it, gift wrapping and all, back in my lap saying, "You can't give me that."

"Why, Frankie?"

He looked at me in disbelief. "Don't you know? You never give a friend a weapon." He had never before referred to me as friend; kid maybe, or even buddy, but never friend. "Wait a minute," he said, fishing in his pocket and coming up with a silver dollar which he placed in my hand. When I protested, he curled my fingers around the silver dollar saying, "You don't understand. I give you a gift at the same time you give me a gift, then it doesn't matter that it's a weapon, and we're still friends. See?"

Maybe old Italian superstitions do work. I still have the silver dollar and, more important, we're still friends.

I went to El Paso to finish my Air Force hitch and didn't hear too much from Frankie for a year. After temporary duty freezing my butt off in Cheyenne, I returned to El Paso in the spring of 1955 to find Frankie and his lady friend, Marcia Edgington, playing clubs in Juarez, Mexico, sister city across the Rio Grande from El Paso. Prior to his arrival, my Juarez nightlife was restricted to serenading 'las senoritas del noche' on tinny bordello pianos with the frequent reward of free beer (popularly known as 'panther piss') from the management, and the infrequent reward of an occasional senorita who took pity on a penniless gringo after the sun rose and she was off duty.

In Frankie's company I was back in the glamorous world of show business, rubbing elbows with everyone from a visiting Ed Sullivan and headliners down to the comedians, singers, dancers, and novelty acts who made up the regulars you got to know on a first name basis over fried rice and egg rolls at El Paso's only all-night Chinese restaurant. With combination number three for twelve people you get two extra dishes, although the sweet and sour pork often tasted more like chile picado. This group revolved around a local theatrical agent named Joe Prensky whose friendship, moral support, and anecdotes about local legends would spur Frankie and me to collaborate on our first serious writing project.

Frankie originally had ambitions to be a movie star, but after years of being stereotyped as a villain in B movies, and without any Hollywood prospects, his thoughts turned to becoming America's Federico Fellini, writing, producing, and directing his own brand of 'art film.'

We both had been devotees of the Avenue Theater, New Orleans's first, and for many years only, art film house run by a man named Vie Force and a woman named Katherine Seoul, who captivated me because she looked and sounded like a short Katharine Hepburn (in fact, she was Hepburn's cousin and had been named after her). The theater pioneered the showing of postwar European films replete with the VFW picketing Chaplin and Bolshoi Ballet films as 'Communist', and the Knights of Columbus picketing Anna Magnani's portrayals in De Sica's and Fellini's films as 'immoral.'

Frankie knew me primarily as a pianist, a very presentable prop in his social adventures, and a fun guy to rap with. The only writing he'd seen me do were songs and some special material for various nightclub acts. One night we went to see a marionette act called Sabin and Her Personettes which so enthralled me I had to meet this tall blonde who looked like a Polish countess and whose thirty-inch-high dolls were amazingly lifelike in their construction and performance.

As a child I had worked with marionettes. My brother, sister, and I gave benefits where we often had to carry our equipment miles for want of carfare to the performance. My brother and sister always preferred human dolls, clowns and senoritas and knights in armor, while I had a quirk for creating and operating such entities as Clarence the Dragon who breathed smoke, Taps the Spider who tap-danced on a sheet of glass, and Pete the Penguin for whom I wrote comedy routines.

I met Sabin struggling with a problem I could particularly understand and sympathize with. She was trying to unsnarl a doll's strings which were hopelessly enmeshed in its clothing. I made her a present of my own silver pocketknife from Japan, a duplicate of the one I gave Frankie, complete with folding miniature scissors and a large eyeleted needle, both of which saved the day for the injured doll, a miniature Fred Astaire who made it safely through the next performance with his equally miniature Ginger Rogers.

Columbia Screen Gems had already done a movie

short subject on the act with its lifelike miniature reproductions of famous movie stars and entertainers of the day, but, knowing that an entertainer can rarely suffer from too much publicity, I did a magazine article about the step-by-step construction and technical mysteries of these tiny people and the artist who created them.

It was this article that brought to Frankie's attention the professional level of my writing and photography, for in my early teens I had bought my first press camera in my efforts to escape poverty, and in the ten years since had periodically profited from my photography and journalistic efforts. This became the catalyst for some of our nebulous ideas and hopes. We would co-author screenplays, Frankie would direct them, I would photograph them, and we both might occasionally appear in vignette roles, ala Fellini. We'd decide who would walk up to the podium to accept the Oscars later.

Our first project was inspired by Joe Prensky, the short, elderly, gnarled, Jewish theatrical agent who mother-henned most of the acts in that area, from a visiting Sinatra to the endless parade of voluptuous strippers, which included, somewhere in the middle, Frankie and Marcia. Joe regaled us many an evening long past sunrise with his vast knowledge of local folklore: show biz and historical, Mexican and American, printable and otherwise, often authenticated by faded yellow newspaper clippings and artifacts ranging from prehistoric fossils to a modem piece of male anatomy in a bottle of formaldehyde on his desk.

Joe had come to El Paso in the twenties as a journalist from Chicago to cover Pancho Villa's raid on the Mexican city of Juarez across the river from El Paso. Joe had been smitten by more than just the excitement of peering from behind barricades on the banks of the Rio Grande at a real shooting war within eyesight, earshot, and gunshot across the river. He succumbed to the lure of blue skies and wide open spaces and, I suspect most of all, his instinct for the vast potential growth in this sleepy area. His instincts rarely failed to turn a coin and we could only guess at the extent of his empire, which we knew to include several copper mines, a glass factory, and dozens of other enterprises covering several states. However, this didn't keep him from running the southwest's largest ticket and theatrical booking agency in a dusty old downtown office lined with racks selling used, dog=eared, sexy paperback books and men's magazines.

His instincts spoke kindly of us, too; more than merely appreciating that we were an enraptured audience for his tales, he was delighted when we researched his stories to find the authentication we felt we needed. For Frankie had decided we would write a television western series about Pancho Villa, changing him into a lovable Robin Hood with certain virtues, ideals, and ethics history never actually found in him. Joe lent me the ancient typewriter he had brought from Chicago forty years before, I scoured every available library for every book I could find on the subject, and we were soon ready to beatify Villa.

Frankie and I traveled into Chihuahua, Mexico, to visit Villa's old stomping grounds, pay our fifty cents to walk through his home, and buy postcards from one of his alleged wives. In the little town of Perral there were men, often barefoot and riding bareback for want of such luxuries as boots and saddles, who still wore gun belts and six-shooters. Villa was a legendary hero there in an arid place where little grew and there was nothing to alleviate the oppressive poverty. The spirit of the people was reflected in the painfully morbid religious carvings in their churches, and the cruelty and sadism that were part of Villa's atrocities seemed to be part and parcel of their image of a hero.

We came back somewhat sobered, but, with unquenchable rationalism, decided that if Hollywood could

9

make a good guy of Wyatt Earp and a macho he-man of Doc Holliday, then we could overlook a little torturing, raping, and town razing in Villa's case. And so was born *The Legends of Pancho Villa*, replete with stirring theme song and tentative production plans, starring Frankie as Villa and all our immediate circle in continuing roles. We considered Disney as a possible producer.

When it came to writing, Frankie was long on creating situations, initial character development, and gag lines. He was short, however, on plot, pace, and resolution, and that is where I complimented his considerable talents. In addition, I contributed a cinematic sense that came from an upbringing in a family of talented people who perceived and analyzed everything in terms of line and form, perspective and motion, color and sound.

By the time Frankie and Marcia had to move on to their Hollywood bookings, we had completed ten scenarios and struggled through the initial shooting script of the introductory pilot. I say struggled because Frankie's idea of collaboration was lying on the sofa dictating an endless series of vignettes to me until he'd get stumped and say, "Then get them out of there," whereupon he'd embark upon another series of vignettes, assuming that in the other sixteen to twenty hours of my day I would "smooth out the rough spots" and "put everything in order." If I were tactless enough to suggest that an episode with only twenty-two minutes program time could not sustain seven comedy bits in a row and still be an action series unless we cast the Three Stooges in it, Frankie would suddenly get a gastritis attack or pick a fight with Marcia.

So I learned to shut up and do it as I saw best, defending myself against "you destroyed my material" by trying to find more appropriate slots for the excess comedy bits in subsequent installments. Frankie would knot his bushy eyebrows over my revised draft and say, "That sounds familiar, but I don't remember doing it yesterday."

"That's just the way you gave it to me, Frankie," and I'd bite my tongue on the thought, "six weeks ago," as he rolled his eyes and turned to the next page. But the series was good, and still is today, even though it's never been done as a series, although Frankie has borrowed from it for other things through the years.

While Frankie and Marcia set up house in Hollywood, I settled down to finish my last year of Air Force service in El Paso, during which I completed two more shooting scripts and ten expanded scenarios to round out a presentation album on the Villa series. Three albums to be exact; one for Frankie, one for me, and one for distribution, which immediately got lost at MCA and we never saw it again.

In between I did a lot of sideline things in show business. I wrote some original songs for Tony Craig, the mutual friend who formerly went with Lee Sharon. A truly talented singer, Tony grew up in Greenwich Village and struggled for a career like his childhood friend, Enzo Stuarte (Tony's family name was Caridi). But, after a booking of several years at Juarez's leading nightclub, La Fiesta, he became concerned about the gray in his temples and words like 'security' and, just before Enzo made it big, Tony became a cruise director with an Italian steamship line and did well enough in little over a decade to retire comfortably to Santa Barbara.

I did promotional materials and musical or special comedy materials for some of the acts, barely breaking even economically, as they would often pay me by picking up my entertainment tabs or the ladies would beguile me with their charms (although I never minded being beguiled if they ladies were charming enough).

One of Joe Prensky's ladies in need was Dolores, who in size, build, and blondness was as Amazonian as Lili St. Cyr, a six foot tall leading stripper of that era, but Dolores' career in no way equalled Lili's. Dolores needed

11

a shrink more than a writer or promoter. Our efforts to map out her career were more like psychosexual therapy sessions with me in the role of analyst, sex-surrogate, and brotherly conspirator in her flights of fantasy fulfillment.

I met her one night when Joe took me to her private dressing room in a Juarez club. The dressing room had been one of her demands of the management as most of the women shared a communal one, and it consisted of two flimsy plywood partitions hastily thrown up in the corner of the club's large kitchen. When we entered the kitchen, the cooks, waiters, cocktail waitresses, and Mexican strippers were all circled around Dolores' dressing room astounded by the earthquake like vibration of its walls and the locomotive sounds that emanated from within.

Suddenly one wall fell outward under the stress of a chair leaned against it in which Dolores was spread-eagled to the utmost limits to accommodate a dark hairy Mexican muscle builder type. He continued his snorting copulative movements which were now accompanied by the clatter of pots and the crash of china trapped under the fallen partition. Most astounding to me was the transfixed attention of the mute audience, some dozen people, who did not respond with a single word or movement to the total, passionate concentration of the two very heathy people, who by this time had also flattened the chair without losing their locomotive rhythm.

Finally, with a sound the likes of which I have only heard in slaughterhouses, the Mexican threw his head back and the muscles of his neck, like the muscles on the inside of her long and well formed thighs, corded so intensely I feared their blood vessels would rupture. The pace of his pounding did not let up, but the sound of it smacked a little wetter. As the pitch of his wail lowered to staccato intakes of air, he slowed to a stop and lay still on top of her, their tan and alabaster skins glistening with the sheen of fine perspiration, their eyes closed.

12

No one moved or made a sound. Joe and I looked at each other and silently raised our hands, as if first seeking approval from each other, and applauded. With a brief pause, not unlike the final curtain of a good play, the stupefied audience woke up and began to applaud as well, until a cook banged a spoon on a pot and ordered everyone back to work.

The muscleman was cool. With his eyes still closed, only a slight smirk betrayed his awareness of the circumstances. Dolores, however, was truly absorbed in her passion and only with the sound of applause did her eyes open to the full situation. As the muscleman rose and, with his back to us, calmly began dressing, Dolores shrieked, "Oh shit!" and, grabbing a robe, dashed into a nearby bathroom.

Within a week she confided to me that the muscleman, a boxer of some note, was her fulfillment of a longstanding desire to make it with a gorilla. In ways she did resemble Fay Wray.

Her other sexual fantasies were, contrary to those of most strippers I've known, not exhibitionist. She didn't want to make it in sight of a policeman, on the steps of a retirement home, or in a pool overlooked by a huge apartment complex. The closest to that behavior was her habit of phoning other people while she was having sex, but that was her sort of one-to-one revenge on individuals who had tried to be possessive of her as the price for their material gifts.

Actually, Dolores's fantasies were rather simple and understandable. She was a big woman, almost six feet, well proportioned but large boned, and dancing every night made her exquisitely formed muscles hard as rock. She had reached that stature when she was little more than thirteen. There had been few if any opportunities for her to experience a man swooping her off her feet. She usually did the swooping. Dolores's fantasy was to be dominated;

13

by a priest, by a Gestapo officer, by her father, by Pancho Villa, by King Kong. Instead of challenging authority figures like most other strippers I had known, she wanted to submit to them.

Though I am inclined to be slightly dominant, it is in a benevolent fatherly fashion, firm but fondly. So we had to make some compromises. It had to be a trade-off rather than a violent act. If she were a nun, it had to be to purge her of her own secret desire. If she were my daughter, it had to be an initiation she herself provoked. If she were Sheena Queen of the Jungle, she owed me for saving her from the elephant stampede.

Whether or not I fully succeeded in making a woman who was as tall as me (taller in heels and hairdo), and damn near as strong, feel petite and helpless, I feel quite sure I made her feel desirable and wanted and happily exhausted at times. Perhaps more important, she felt she wasn't the only person 'bizarre' enough to explore her own feelings and imagination.

Not the least of my reward was the sweet revenge against my military environment as Dolores would drive me through more than one reveille formation in her brand new 1956 pink Thunderbird convertible to drop me off at work, where my gawking bosses could overhear, "Bye bye, Daddy," or "Good morning, Father Rabelais," or "Sheena loves King Kong."

Another act that hit town was Johnny Aladdin, born John Randall, whom Frankie and I had known in New Orleans's French Quarter where, in addition to his magician-hypnotist-escape artist nightclub act, he had appeared together with Frankie in several episodes of *NOPD* (New Orleans Police Department), a locally produced television series. Johnny was always playing a heavy, his James Cagney tough guy exterior largely coming from Frankie's tutoring while Frankie's tough-guy exterior leaned towards Leo Gorcey.

14

Though Johnny was perhaps the shortest of us all and several years older than the oldest of us, he was an amazingly imposing figure. I later came to learn this was a product of his ghetto upbringing and an exceptional instinct for psychology. He worshiped Harry Houdini and had accomplished most of his feats. His dedication to the rigorous physical training required of an escape artist gave him an impressive physique and lithe sense of timing to his presence. The aura Johnny created around himself was a mystique, a conscious theatrical creation on his own part.

Prior to this I had been interested enough to read and study the occult, spiritism, Houdini, and hypnotism. While with the Air Force in the Orient, I had produced and performed in shows that included oriental hypnotists who shared some of their expertise with me. I did not respect most popularized stage applications of hypnotism, but through their generosity broadened my knowledge of the subject enough to practice hypnosis therapeutically for some of my friends.

Though Johnny and I had been acquainted previously in the French Quarter, we did not know each other well enough to discover our mutual interests until we found ourselves together as part of El Paso's small coterie of American entertainers. When Johnny saw the completed *Legends of Pancho Villa*, it led to our collaboration on *The Adventures of Johnny Aladdin*, a contemporary adventure series about an entertainer modeled after Johnny who, together with his agent friend acting as comedic sidekick, travel around the world getting into action and romance filled intrigues. I loved the format, and with the experience of writing the Villa series, plus the fact that Johnny's principal collaborative interest was in providing expertise on magicianship and 'in' secrets of the profession, I found that the writing flowed.

I finished the series before leaving the service and El Paso, and after Johnny had gone to Japan to fulfill a series of bookings there. Again, there were three presentation albums with three shooting scripts, ten scenarios, stirring theme song, and promo materials, one of which was immediately lost by the Will Morris Agency.

In the meantime, while I was still in El Paso, I got a letter from Frankie describing Hollywood as the town "which will be our oyster." His enthusiasm about our future writing projects and his new friend and talent discovery, Lenny Bruce, was immensely encouraging, although I almost felt like a faithless wife, having just finished a series with Johnny in half the time it took Frankie and I to write *Villa.* But I looked forward with gusto to my emancipation from the Air Force and a glamorous career as a Hollywood screenwriter. Frankie and I had always relished oysters, preferably on the half shell.

Chapter 2
HOORAY FOR HOLLYWOOD

Great moments of insight and inspiration require the coincidence of both the exceptional perception of the beholder and the exceptional performance of the subject beheld. I often wonder if the subject of Jesus or Buddha or Mohammed was always exceptional, if they did indeed require potty training or succumb to fleshly weaknesses or ever fully reach a state of total infallibility. If they had an off day, could the most perceptive individual around them still recognize that here was a talented and perceptive spokesman for all humanity?

Thus I rationalize the fact that, when I first met Lenny, I did not recognize his immense talent and potential. Whether or not this was a momentary lack in Lenny and/or me, what is immensely important in my life is that we both eventually recognized each other's ability and experienced the fruits and joys of collaboration.

Late in 1956, while still in the service and after completing both the Villa and Aladdin series, I took a furlough to join Frankie in Hollywood and initiate further writing projects. As I pulled my dusty sun-bleached 1949 Chevy off the Hollywood Freeway at Sunset Boulevard, I was confronted by the same sea of soft drink and movie bill- boards I had left in El Paso, but the noonday sun shimmering off those billboards and buildings struck me as the aura of a promised land.

Fulfillment of that promise then seemed a short step beyond the sound of Frankie's sleepy voice over the phone and the subsequent appearance of Marcia's beautiful alabaster face framed in natural red hair as she drove down to meet me and guide me to their apartment near Fairfax and Santa Monica Boulevard. I was ensconced in a hotel three doors from the intersection, a hotel so inconspicuous you didn't know it was there until you stepped into a recessed doorway, saw the faded sign that declared "Rooms" in turn-of-the-century lettering, and looked up a foreboding stairway. The rent was ten bucks a week and would have been no bargain at any price. I left my valuables at Frankie's and only used the hotel room to sleep.

After giving me the grand tour of Hollywood Boulevard (it was cleaner then), Sunset Strip (it was tamer then), and the all-night delis where the 'show biz peep' congregated, Frankie and Marcia took me to meet Frankie's talented new friend, Lenny Bruce.

Lenny was working in an obscure burlesque with a half-hearted Polynesian decor, a small, undistinguished lineup of girls, and, by the end of the first show, an audience that consisted of only one other couple besides our table (for all I know, the other couple may have been friends of the management).

I cannot remember one thing Lenny did. At the time I was impressed only that someone could stay on stage that long without finishing a single routine. For the most part, I found his monologue unintelligible, and what was intelligible revolved around in-jokes between Lenny and Frankie. To make it even worse, only Lenny laughed at them.

Lenny was very thin with dark circles under his eyes in an already dark face, looking as jaded as Marcia had described him to me. I was very fond of Marcia, a beautiful woman and warm person whose wonderful sense of humor was often very creative, but I had guessed that most of Marcia's disapproval of Lenny was jealousy over his closeness to Frankie.

Frankie was chagrined by the poor performance he had brought me to witness, and further embarrassed when

Lenny ignored his introduction to me while joining us at the table. Later that night I had to convince Frankie I was not offended, and Marcia was as smugly happy as the Cheshire cat that Lenny had been so singularly unimpressive. When Frankie asked what I had seen in Lenny, all I could honestly say was a possible hypothyroid case who couldn't focus his talent to his best advantage. However, I reasoned largely in behalf of Frankie's interest in Lenny, an overactive thyroid might well be an asset for two guys like Frankie and me with barely normal ones.

I saw a lot of Lenny when he came to rap with Frankie before and after their respective 9 p.m. to 2 a.m. gigs, Frankie's at the Near and Far on Santa Monica Boulevard, and Lenny's at Duffy's Gay Nineties on Cahuenga just south of Franklin, and which later became a Greek restaurant. Both were strip joints of the lowest order, what are commonly called 'toilets' among entertainers.

The Near and Far was just around the comer from Frankie's apartment and, though Frankie could and previously did play quality rooms at far better money, he found the Near and Far a convenient steady gig while trying to remain in Hollywood to promote a writing career.

For Lenny, however, Duffy's was a different kind of compromise. Though he had played all across the country while traveling with his wife Honey, a beautiful exotic dancer who was currently serving a drug rap at nearby San Pedro, I suspect Lenny had burned some professional bridges behind him and had little choice but to work at Duffy's.

The owner of Duffy's was affectionately known as Rocky and, whether it was just a pose or reality, he was the stereotype of the broken-nosed, gravel-voiced retired bad guy from Chicago, which in fact was his home town. Rocky loved Lenny and would let him work there for $125 a week whenever Lenny couldn't find work elsewhere, which turned out to be for months on end when I met him.

Most of the lineup onstage at Duffy's was 'coasting' for want of a better gig, and half the girls were hookers who were not paid to dance, but did it simply as an opportunity to solicit in the club, turning their tricks at the several nearby hotels or even right at, on, or under the tables in the club's mezzanine seating area.

Duffy's was also a heavy drug scene at a time when drugs were a heavy social and legal trip. Typical was Lenny's oldest and most intimate friend, Joe Maini, a thin pallid hook-nosed clarinetist of exceptional musical talent, who abdicated any serious musical career in favor of being a pimp and a pusher to support his habit. Joe and his girlfriend Sandra would go to bizarre and pathetic lengths to support their habit, such as a mock wedding they performed on stage at Duffy's with Sandra eight months pregnant by some unknown john and the bandleader officiating, all for the purpose of hocking the resulting wedding gifts to buy dope.

This ranked among the high points at Duffy's, along with the evening Lenny appeared nude and urinated in a knothole on the stage floor, about which the dancers had complained because they caught their spike heels in it. Lenny explained the act as a labor protest on the girls' behalf, but I was told he'd done the same thing in other clubs for nothing more than shock value.

During my first two-week visit to Hollywood in 1956, Lenny was either aloof or condescending to me because I was ten years younger than he and Frankie. But Lenny was curiously observant of the manner in which I helped Frankie regiment the writing program and fulfill specific goals and deadlines. During that two weeks we scripted a feature art film entitled *Lygie,* short for Elijah, a Felliniesque story about a small black boy's various misadventures among the beauties and the beasts of New Orleans's French Quarter. It was a very good script and

20

Lenny was obviously impressed.

But Lenny made no real overtures to me until I returned in the spring of 1957, after leaving the service, and started writing *Playhouse 90* kinds of stories with Frankie, who was on a biography kick. First we did the life of Pete Herman, world bantamweight champion who went blind at the height of his boxing career, yet later became a successful nightclub owner in the French Quarter. Frankie and I knew him well, and Johnny Aladdin, who had worked for Pete for several years, shared many anecdotes about him with us.

The second biography was about Nick Lucas, America's first big- time vocalist of the new recording industry and early talking pictures. Lucas was still alive then, and we interviewed him in his San Fernando Valley home, saw the rare early sound movie prints some of which had color tinted sequences, and viewed his last film, *Tiptoe Through The Tulips,* which employed one of the first full-color processes. It is an amazing story about a man who was the first at the top of a new industry, one of the very first superstars about whom Bing Crosby once said, "I wouldn't be here if Nick Lucas hadn't stepped down." Yet the very enormity of his success frightened Nick Lucas into retirement. It was during the writing of the Nick Lucas story that, for want of a better term, Lenny began to court me.

I was working for a publicist named Sam Wall, a job Tony Craig had set up for me before I left El Paso. Tony had an old flame living in Paris who was a jet-setter ex-wife of a vice-presidential candidate. Tony referred me to her when I was temporarily stationed in England and knew I'd be visiting Paris. We met and spent a weekend, then corresponded after my return to the States. Upon learning I needed a job in Hollywood, she wrote to have Tony introduce me to her sister, who used to be a child star in the *Our Gang* comedy series and whose husband, Sam, was a publicist who would employ me.

Sam used to handle the top celebrities and was the principal model for *Sweet Smell of Success,* a less than admirable image which he was nonetheless proud of. He had phased out handling celebrities, with the exception of Ernest Borgnine and two others, preferring instead to specialize in top-name restaurants, which offered the dual advantage of prompter payment plus a commodity to bribe journalists with, i.e., free entertainment at prestige restaurants.

This commodity was further negotiable with resort hotels and pretty girls aspiring to stardom. The restaurants would feed the columnist, the starlet, and the manager of the resort hotel, getting publicity in exchange. The hotel manager would provide accommodations for the columnist and starlet, a double of course, and in exchange get entertained at the restaurant and perhaps by the starlet, and some publicity for the resort. Sam would provide publicity for all involved and, in exchange, be paid money by the restaurant and possibly the hotel, and usually more than a pound of flesh by the starlet. Finally, the starlet would entertain the columnist, and most likely one and all, getting nothing but some publicity, unless one counted exhaustion, infrequent trauma, and an occasional dose of something unexpected.

My daily routine started with trying to get Frankie to write with me before I began work with Sam at noon, a real hassle for Frankie who normally slept until then. Marcia was often the ballast that kept us from each other's throats and kept us going. She could make Frankie laugh when he was upset with my editing, and she could rationalize with me when I was frustrated with Frankie's temperament. She kept us amiable by alleviating our hard times with movies, visiting friends, or eating out, feeling that, while it strained the budget, it was an investment in the product we were creating. The majority of the time she displayed a perceptive and creative mind and a warm and generous heart. Besides that, she was a raving beauty, even when she first woke up in the morning.

Around noon, Sam and I would make the rounds of the restaurants, often breakfasting on some inappropriately rich entree being prepared for that evening, and picking up gossip that would become the grains of truth in the blurbs we'd write. After covering La Cienega and Beverly Hills, we'd return to Sam's home above Sunset Strip to write our largely fictional "who was seen, heard, caught at where with whom" on Sam's custom typewriter with large kingprint type. I might have shot some 4" x 5" photos in the afternoon, but more likely, I would shoot them when we'd go to supper at The Captain's Table, Scandia, or, Sam's favorite, Villa Capri.

Frank Sinatra's part ownership of Villa Capri and the likelihood of his presence made it the most fruitful rendezvous for celebrities to glean tidbits from and columnists to give the embroidered product to. One of Sinatra's invaluable assets to his career, which few people might be aware of, is the limitless quantity and quality of his charm when it is professionally expedient to turn it on. I have seen him turn from being less than kind to good and beautiful people in order to woo an ugly, alcoholic, but influential, columnist. It was the magnitude of that charm which Sam liked to follow in the wake of, skimming the fallout for radioactive tidbits.

Yet Sam was tactless enough and, I suspect jealous enough, to proliferate and even initiate juvenile anti-Sinatra jokes and sentiments. "He's so tough I once saw him beat up a crippled newsboy who short-changed him." "He's so sexy he has three chicks at a time. Then, if he can't get it up, they can always play bridge." "He wears those bow ties so you can tell it's him behind the mike stand."

Sam was a tall, balding man, a round shapeless ball

above two long legs. His nose was huge, his chin weak, and his teeth rotten with breath to match. He was born Sam Wallenstein and grew up the hard way in New York City. In himself, he had no redeeming features. He had a wife who was a petite living doll, and they had six children for whom he provided with food by the case. We were invariably spending as much time doing household shopping as taking care of business. To his family he was an excellent provider and, I'm sure in some ways a hero. To the world he was a corrupt publicist-pimp-wheeler-dealer, with nothing to be proud of except his power over little people like starlets and waiters and busboys. Being so close to Sinatra, I'm sure the disparity ate at Sam. Naturally, Sam's barbs against Sinatra were those things Sam himself was likely to be guilty of.

If I witnessed any flaw in Sinatra, it was an illness from which most highly successful people in the business suffered, that of sometimes exhibiting power over little people, possibly to vent the great stress of their positions. One could hardly feel sorry for the beefcake assistants with whom he was sometimes short or gave simpleton errands to as if they were schoolchildren. One of the sturdiest was on his payroll as a "music carrier." But these men were always secure in the knowledge that, if they wanted to, they could braid Sinatra, Sam, and me into a pigtail.

The ones I felt most sorry for were the endless parade of fantastically beautiful women. It's true that many women think they can substitute sex for talent, and by screwing every elf and elephant in the circus they can somehow by association become a star in the center ring. I'm sure some of the women I saw with Sinatra earned the harsh words, the chilling glares, and the demotions to being someone else's 'escort' for the evening. However, there were some I felt were not trying to manipulate or exploit their association with Sinatra, but were truly infatuated, if not actually in love, with the man whose aura was so great it was understandable.

Whatever Sinatra's faults, I, fortunately, did not run afoul of them. The worst I did was back up to the same barstool he did, resulting in bumping bottoms and suffering the most withering glare I've ever seen a person deliver. Thereafter, Sam referred to it as my crowning social contact of the season.

I never had occasion to deal with Sinatra unless he wanted to flatter someone with candid pictures with him, at which times he'd always address me by some name other than my own. I took dozens of pictures of him with dozens of different people, but never managed to have my picture taken with him even for the hell of it.

I did, after all, admire the man, not so much for his vocalizing which, early in his career, I felt left something to be desired, but when *From Here To Eternity* brought him back on the scene, I really sat up and took notice of his acting ability. This occurred shortly after I started working around him and I came to appreciate the depth and diversity of his talent. I was further impressed when, in the middle of his career, he resumed musical studies and ultimately conducted full symphony orchestras in purely instrumental recordings.

As for those he slighted, there were a substantial if not equal number of little people he helped on the way up for the sake of their talent and not because of what they could or did do for him.

Even more frustrating than not being photographed with him was an evening when Tony Craig was in town and at Villa Capri with Sam and me. Tony started rapping with Sinatra about mutual friends in the business and Sam suggested that Tony sing for Sinatra, which Sinatra encouraged Tony to do. The regular pianist didn't know Tony's songs or keys, so Sam suggested I accompany him, which I had done many times in Mexico, including working on some of my own songs for recordings we had planned. I began suggesting numbers to Tony and Sinatra said he'd do some of them with him. Tony declined and later confessed to me it was because he was intimidated by the thought of performing for Sinatra. But I lost my chance to say I had accompanied Sinatra and any chance of slipping in a "Hey Tony, let Frank hear some of the numbers I wrote for your Mexico City album." Such are the whims of fate.

If I managed to get home before midnight, I'd try to rework what Frankie Ray and I'd written, if anything, that morning, then join him at the Near and Far before closing, in vain hope of scoring with a dancer, waitress, cigarette girl, or rare female customer. The truth is, a burlesque house is the most unlikely place in the world to score, especially for a pauper.

After work we'd frequently end up at one of the all night delis on Fairfax or the Strip. Canter's may still be one of the favorite rendezvous of show biz people and hangers-on in the after hours. Canter's was the most significant location in my personal education regarding show business, and I liked the food.

At that time, poor Cohen next door was still in business, or, at least, he was still open for business, but the place was empty and the help would stand at the window watching the crowds going into Canter's. I tried to analyze their success, as did many who watched it snowball through the years, until Canter finally bought Cohen out and made Cohen's into an annex for Canter's overflow. I finally decided, although everybody else had some different theory, that, besides the inherent advantage in the superb bakery on the premises, the recent renovations made the place look like a theater which drew in show people who in turn drew in crowds.

It had a theater marquee complete with delta overhang and flashing white and yellow lights, a low-ceilinged foyer where the bakery and deli counters were indirectly lit like refreshment counters in a theater, and a display window sat like a ticket box flanked by double doors on each side. The high-ceilinged interior seating area was stepped and laid out rather like a theater in the round so guests could decide whether they wanted to be part of the audience or part of the cast. We usually elected to be in the audience in one of the large round booths to the side and the rear.

Here would congregate a sideshow collection of strippers, comedians, musicians, agents, club owners, cocktail waitresses, hookers who hadn't scored yet that evening, pimps waiting for those who had, movie bit players who lived on the edge of the business, and occasional celebrities out slumming. All were summoned at the Cinderella hour of two in the morning by California's alcohol license laws.

Here was the professional marketplace where performers were looking for agents or vice versa, agents and performers were looking for work from club owners, club owners were sometimes looking for girls not necessarily to perform on stage, and the girls were looking for that magic 'contact' that would help them graduate into the movies or some equally lucrative good fortune which would enable them to "get out of the business."

The news of the day centered around who was opening, who was closing, who had arrived in town, who was leaving on tour, and the cost and quality of tailoring, costume making, music arranging, music copyists, wigs, toupees, cosmetics, beauticians, health parlors, travel fares, hotel rates, special material, publicity, and the countless other services and products needed to bolster a successful theatrical career. Many of the conversations sounded like a mutual challenge to see who had read the daily trade papers most thoroughly, and Frankie was almost never a loser on that score.

Lenny would always egg Frankie on to tell

anecdotes about celebrities Frankie had known, for Frankie had worked with practically all of them at one time or another. Lenny was particularly interested in their faux pas, their weaknesses and liabilities, which ones had nose jobs, bust jobs, and hairpieces, which ones were gay, which ones had been busted and for what. Lenny had come into maturity on the brink of the post World War II social revolution and wanted proof that the establishment was a deserving target, even if the establishment in this case were those more successful in show business.

I learned about the evolution of hairpieces; the relative merits of synthetics, horsehair, or the finest being women's hair imported from Italy, the virtues and liabilities of good and bad nets, surgically implanted fasteners, and surgically implanted hair. I learned that the first big-time bust surgeon was a German who firmly believed the best foam rubber implants were made from the seat cushions of Messerschmidt fighter planes; that Japanese surgeons pioneered the wax injections which they also used in cosmetic eyelid surgery on oriental women; and that some drag queens used silicone in search of rounder faces and tushes.

Lenny would always pump me for details about the celebrities I was around while working for Sam. Fortunately for me, the first incident I related to him was innocuous enough and taught me to be guarded about confidences thereafter. I was surrounded by vicious gossip in the publicity game and felt that using anecdotes in storytelling should oblige one to achieve a broader perspective or lesson with them, and not at the expense, much less the injury, of another. Besides, I didn't want one of Sinatra's assistants visiting me unofficially,

The incident was innocent enough and involved an aspiring starlet from one of the many showcase theaters that Sam cultivated for just such girls, Cabaret Concert Theater on Sunset, the Music Hall Theater on Hollywood at La Brea, the Los Palmas Theater, Billy Grey's Band Box on Fairfax, and many others were producing equity plays or variety shows like *The Billy Barnes Revue* or the endless string of Billy Grey satires like *My Fairfax Lady.* Most of them barely broke even, flooding the studio publicity and casting departments with complimentary tickets and hoping to pay the expenses with the food sold in their restaurant-theater format, all for the opportunity to practice and sharpen their craft and showcase their talents to the industry,

Sam was welcomed as an influential publicist and traded publicity for the services of those girls pretty enough, and willing enough, to visit the casting couch. In most cases the management was at worst a naive partner in the transaction, often believing the complimentary tickets and food they provided for columnists was what gained the publicity they received, although they must have wondered at times how a pretty but mediocre actress got the lion's share of that publicity.

Beverly was a statuesque blonde with a baby face and cantilevered bosom, ideal for the female lead in *Will Success Spoil Rock Hunter,* which she was doing at the Music Hall Theater. Actually, I had stopped by the theater during the performance to transact some business with my friend, John Neris, who was playing the role of the agent. John was 5'1" tall and had been bald since he was twenty, so his impressive acting talents were relegated to character roles like the little French photographer he played in the movie *Can Can* and dozens of others like that. John earned his principal living teaching one or more of the seven languages he spoke fluently at Los Angeles City College and other nearby campuses. In this play he was typically cast, his 5'1" a perfect comedy foil for Beverly's spike-heeled 6'2."

Sam hadn't been to the theater in months and didn't want to take the time to stop, so he was pacing around nervously, waiting to use the backstage pay phone while I talked to John who was momentarily offstage. Just as Sam got possession of the phone and dropped the dime in, he spied Beverly jiggling offstage to wait in the wings for her next entrance. I could tell Sam was impressed because he walked six feet toward Beverly before remembering to return and retrieve his dime, by which time she had made another stage entrance.

Sam, who had always before been turned off by John's impeccable manners and diction, suddenly greeted him like a long lost brother and surprised me by inviting John to join us as his guest at Villa Capri after the show and added, "By the way, why don't you bring that tall blonde girl there with you so we can discuss the publicity potentials for the cast as well as the production." As Sam turned his drooling attention to Beverly onstage, I shrugged while John gave me a knowing take, sighed, and said, "I'm sure Beverly will appreciate a free meal just as much as I know I shall."

As Sam and I waited at Villa Capri, I was pleased to see Sinatra was in an exceptionally good mood. Anna Magnani was dining there for the first time. Mature by then, her feisty youthful image had mellowed into a handsome though matronly woman, albeit her hair shone unnaturally black and her exquisite floor-length black lace dress sported a provocative neckline. She conversed in French and Italian with the two distinguished looking gray-haired gentlemen at her table, and, from the smattering of French I could understand, the glamorous setting was devoted to discussing the trials and tribulations of being a pet owner and trying to find competent domestics in Beverly Hills.

I watched Sinatra wait for the appropriate moment during after- dinner coffee to introduce himself, addressing her briefly in Italian I knew to be salutary openers. Then I empathized with him as, in English, he expressed respect for her immense talents and appreciation for the understanding she had given the world of the role of women, Catholics, and Italians during the postwar period. I empathized because I shared those sentiments and could not imagine them delivered by a more impressive source nor in a manner more charming yet humble and, I firmly believe, sincere.

By the time Anna Magnani left and John entered with Beverly, Sinatra was exuberantly happy and seated in a center table with Patsy D' Amore, principal owner of the restaurant. John and Beverly made an eye-stopping pair for a lot of obvious reasons, but Sinatra's double-take was obviously focused on her physique and particularly its upper elevations. Overheard as far as our booth, but untranslatable to Beverly, were his flattering but earthy expletives.

The usual followed, with an assistant from Sinatra asking Sam over to speak to Sinatra, followed by an invitation for us to join him while he listened politely but briefly to Beverly and John's career status and ambitions. John had not yet worked with Sinatra, but mentioned meeting him by way of a three second handshake while an army private overseas when Sinatra had done troop shows years before. Ten minutes later, after taking their names and numbers, Sinatra retreated to another room only long enough for us to be returned to our booth so he could reclaim his table.

It was ironic that, though John's name and number probably went in the round file immediately, he ended up working with Sinatra several times through entirely different and more professional routes. Though Beverly saw Sinatra personally several times immediately following the introduction, to my knowledge she never worked with Sinatra nor do I know if the few parts in 'B' films she worked in after that were in any way obtained through her contact with him.

This incident, told in confidence to Lenny, not only immediately became public knowledge, but got blown out of all proportion, with me coming off like a superpimp, Beverly as a moronic round-heeled pushover, and John and Sam like a gallery of freaky voyeurs. After that, lechers offered me money to use my 'publicity routine' to get them starlets who were not hardened hookers. Hardened hookers offered me sex to get them into the movies. And celebrity enamored women, more commonly known as 'starfuckers,' offered me money and/or sex to get them assignations with stars. Lenny thought it was hilarious, Sam thought it was the natural order of things, and I thought it was sickening that the smut had rubbed off on me.

I played it cool thereafter when Lenny periodically played one of his favorite games of having everyone at the booth in Canter's tell the name and circumstances of the biggest star they had gone to bed with. Most of the claims were bullshit, some were true as I later learned, and at least one story was comical.

Frankie made the mistake of confessing his most illustrious conquest in his early years on the East coast, a lady of longstanding international fame, but the farthest from being a sex symbol that could be imagined. It was not that she was older (she had to be pretty young at the time), but let's just say she was far from being slim. Everyone forgot that Frankie had numerous relationships spanning years with more than one of the most beautiful women in the business, and for years was made sport of for one lone incident confessed to one night in Canter's at Lenny's prodding.

But Lenny was not necessarily cruel, nor did he strike out blindly in reflex to everything that came his way. Rather, he was like a child, constantly testing authority and being amazed by its incongruities. Many of his mannerisms were childlike, from his spontaneous, high-pitched, slightly hysterical laughter to his hushed confiding tones when, his eyes appearing all the larger in his swarthy face, he would share the revelation of some social illogic which all the world had always known but never thought of in that light. The distinction in Lenny was that, though the revelation might be the basis of a joke, it was never the basis of despair.

I never had children, but being around Lenny was somewhat like the relearning process one experiences with a child's growing discoveries. Witnessing Lenny's ecstatic, humorous, and intensely sincere discoveries of the sweet and sometimes bittersweet mysteries of life helped me learn anew, more deeply and honestly, the meanings and motives of life.

Lenny was always in the learning process, a blessed state I feel I've come by partly through intellect, and one which I suspect Lenny came by through glandular imbalance, compulsively exploring and gleefully discovering like a hyper-active child. Everyone he spent time with became either tutor or test case to his interests, and I learned to be the former to avoid the sometimes uncomfortable consequences of being the latter. I learned this right from the start because the first thing I did for Lenny was a kind of tutoring, and he was an apt pupil, but the second thing was disastrous for me and almost cost me my job.

The first thing was to take professional pictures for Lenny because, until then, he never had anything but studio mug shots which, if you're handsome as Lenny was, always make you look nice and that's all; no fencing, no tension, no dimension. When I do photography, still or cine, I pursue all the alternatives leading to the primary objectives and any unknown objectives those alternatives many reveal. I deal with subjects like a theatrical director hoping to achieve a rapport with them and elicit those responses I initially desire and those hidden within them which quite often they desire.

It was this approach that turned Lenny on as we did his pictures in my Bronson Avenue apartment, having graduated from the hotel on Santa Monica and Fairfax to a 'bachelor' consisting of one room with bath, and a hotplate located in the cubbyhole the Murphy bed folded into. As I adjusted lamps fashioned from coffee cans and tin foil and peered into my Japanese copy of a Korelle 2 1/4" x 2 1/4" single lens reflex camera acquired while serving in the Orient, I started a casual but probing dialogue designed to hypnotize the subject into a sense of security and intimacy.

Lenny immediately sensed what I was doing and it blew his mind.

He had never seen me take the dominant role in the creative process before. He had never really sat in while Frankie and I wrote, he had never been around Sam and me at work, and he had never (and ultimately never did) seen me perform as a musician or before an audience, although he eventually saw me do bit parts in our movies to his amazement.

What followed was an orgy of creative discussion. Lenny was a person you don't have to seduce into creativity, he would jump into it with both feet quicker than he'd jump into bed with a beautiful woman, and he'd do that quicker than most. Typically, his mind leaped ahead to ambitious and bizarre regions beyond the technical, financial, and time limits we were working with. He asked me to do everything with him: write, manage, produce, nightclubs, records, films. He was like a woman who wants to move in with you after the first encounter, flattering but frightening.

I reined him back to reality and made the following propositions. I understood Frankie to be more or less managing him and I wouldn't infringe on that relationship, but would aid and abet Frankie's efforts where I could with publicity, bookings, and contacts. I would write with him on a fifty-fifty basis after I had finished the current Nick Lucas project with Frankie. I would contribute photography, cinematography, sound engineering, and other production expertise to co-productions in exchange for expense money and deferred payment contracts for those specific functions performed, including co-producer if those functions were multiple. For starters, because he couldn't pay me for the stills we were then shooting, I'd let him pay me with the modeling services for one sitting if he would accept the premise of the photos I had in mind.

The premise evolved around strong feelings I had about the number thirty-three. I was born in 1933. In high school I impressed a teacher with a thesis about the metaphysical implications of the numeral three (proton-neutron-electron, male-female-procreated life, the Holy Trinity, etc.). I developed a premonition that I would reach a zenith of success at the age of thirty-three.

At the time we shot those pictures, Lenny was thirty-three and I brought to his attention that Jesus was thirty-three at the peak of his life. Furthermore, Jesus, like Lenny, was a Jew who invoked the wrath and disdain of his own people, for if Lenny had any limited recognition at that time it was as a 'dirty Jewish comic,' which incensed the large Jewish middle-class society in Hollywood.

I proposed to Lenny that he pose for me as Jesus on the cross as soon as I had appropriate studio space to work in, and that we explore creating a dramatic, charismatic image for him which the pictures we shot that day only began to reflect. I posed him with a gun, with a knife, and with the intent to delineate his arched eyebrows and character lines rather than pluck and smooth them. Lenny loved what we did that day and ardently promised to model as I had requested, a promise he would renege on with his first success and years later finally revoke.

It was that first photo sitting that molded our

collaborative association and the messianic image of himself Lenny began to adopt.

The second thing I did for Lenny I did without asking anything in return, and it all but shook loose my tenuous foothold in the upper strata of Hollywood.

The Slate Brothers, a three-man comedy team whose movie career spanned the thirties and forties, were opening a posh new nightclub on La Cienega, replete with crystal chandeliers, mirrored walls, and carpet so deep it would shine your shoes in six steps. Sam's first chore, as the club's publicist, was to dream up a fantastic opening show for short money. At the time, I was more in the swim of nightclub acts than Sam, particularly the inexpensive acts, so he stood me up in front of the Slate Brothers as the authority on the subject. I sold them on an up-and-coming jazz quintet I believed in, a young vocalist who was the student of a vocal coach who in turn was the husband of one of my models, and an up-and-coming comic named Lenny Bruce who I tried to convince them was almost as 'zany' as they used to be in the movies.

This would be Lenny's first class booking, to my knowledge, in Hollywood, and he had a two-week contract with six weeks of options and salary increases. Frankie and I groomed him like a fighter for the title. I researched the Slate Brothers movies and favorite shticks, and Frankie wrote material related to them and the potential guests at the opening, all of which Lenny spumed. He was miffed at the low pay, he was aesthetically opposed to the Slate Brothers and their brand of comedy, and he was scared of the posh room.

The celebrity lineup in the audience didn't help Lenny's nerves opening night. It was a Hollywood 'who's who' of who-you-didn't-want- to and I-couldn't-afford-to offend. I was grateful Sinatra wasn't there, for Sam would surely have blamed me for anything that went wrong, but to replace Sinatra in my anxiety at that moment was

George Raft, seated in the center of the rear wall with his arm around six beautiful women, three on either side of him.

The first show, Lenny was just nervous. When a line failed, he'd turn his back on the audience and play to the band, all jazz musicians he knew personally and who dug his brand of humor. He couldn't hide his disdain for the Slate Brothers. When his own material didn't go over, he'd try one of our researched bits about the owners and, somehow, it would come out like a slur against them. The audience laughter, prompted at first by a claque consisting of me, Sam, the Slate Brothers, and their staff, began to dwindle to sporadic, polite responses and finally nervous titters at Lenny's obvious discomfort.

After the first show, one of the Slate Brothers came over to Sam and said, "Can't you revive him? He's dying up there." As he left, Sam turned grimly to me and said, "He's your baby and I think he needs his diaper changed."

Frankie was working at the Near And Far and called between shows to inquire, congratulate, and cheer Lenny, but I had to take Lenny out back and try to reason with him that he had two weeks to acclimate to the room and all he had to worry about that night was not to make any serious mistakes, and just stick to his routines we had previously selected and the segues we had written for him. But Lenny wouldn't listen.

The second show was a disaster. When he couldn't get the audience started at all, he digressed with a grossly sick joke Buddy Hackett had told us the previous night at Canter's where it had only drawn nervous laughter from an all male group.

"Daddy, what's a pervert?"

"Shut up, son, and keep sucking."

There was cataclysmic silence, broken only by the sound of a Slate brother accidentally spitting a drink into the face of the bartender and clattering his way off a bars tool to head straight for our table like a man with diarrhea running a footrace. While Lenny began to verbally attack the Slate Brothers and the guests, suggesting that the six women with George Raft were hookers and no strangers to fellatio, and that the famous Broadway star in the front row acquired her large mouth by practicing it too much, Slate began a tirade against Sam who was already pointing his finger at me saying, "He hired him."

This Slate brother (I can't remember their individual names, but they were all red-headed and tough-looking bozos) grabbed my shirtfront and pulled me to a half-standing position so that, though I was taller, he was still looking directly down into my face. "Get that garbage-mouthed bastard off my stage or you and he won't be able to walk, much less work, in this city the rest of your lives."

He threw me violently down in my seat, momentarily making a more entertaining spectacle than Lenny, who continued to berate the audience with barbs about their sexual proclivities and, in rationalization, their capacity for honesty. I was in shock. When George Raft got up to leave with his ladies, I thought he might attack Lenny or, in my paranoia, that somehow he'd heard I was responsible and was coming after me.

I crouched between the tables and made my way to the edge of the stage trying to get Lenny's attention, slashing my throat with my finger to signal him to cut and feeling I had really been garroted. When Lenny chose to ignore me, I pulled on the bandleader's pants leg and silently mouthed, "Play something." As Gil Bernal started some exit music, I stood up smiling and clapping and extended my hand in seeming congratulations to Lenny while a Slate brother entered from the opposite side of the stage, grabbing the mike to applaud and congratulate Lenny who I then pulled bodily offstage and out the door. The next day Lenny made the front page of the trades for the first time: "LENNY BRUCE FIRED FOR BLUE

MATERIAL."

For me it was the beginning of the end as an 'insider.' Thereafter Sam didn't want me to advise clients about anything, although I had become increasingly instrumental in designing client images until then. He wanted to proof everything I wrote for fear, I suspect, I'd put 'dirty' words into it. Where before he trusted me to escort columnists, or deliver copy to their homes or offices without him, sometimes even typing up their column for them if they were too hung over, now he feared I might sell them some bill of goods or try to hustle the contact or account away from him.

To further strain things between Sam and me, he got himself in a financial bind by borrowing a large sum of money from a client. The client was one of the few personality accounts Sam accepted while I was with him. We drove out Wilshire to the high-rise apartment district and entered an expensive apartment staffed with beefcake assistants similar to Sinatra's, but these all wore loud printed sport shirts instead of the fine tailoring seen in the Villa Capri.

We were frisked, which was the first clue I had as to the nature of Sam's new client. I was seated in an outer room with a full view through an open door of the inner sanctum where Sam stood at attention while conversing with a short man who had so little hair he barely needed the barber who was laboring meticulously over him. In the less than one hour we were there, the short man left the room several times to, presumably, wash his hands which I could see him drying upon his return. He was the mobster Mickey Cohen, who had a fetish about washing his hands, the kind of eccentric touch I would have hesitated to give a gangster character in a screenplay.

But Mickey Cohen was a classic stereotype in some ways, and his paranoia about being harassed by the police may not have been entirely imagined. He was incurring an

39

unusually large number of traffic tickets and citations for minor violations. It was common knowledge the local administration did not relish the adverse publicity of having known gangsters in their midst. Mickey felt they were leaning on him, and Sam was the top man skilled in reversing that adverse publicity.

It was such a hush-hush account that I didn't know who the short man was until days later when I heard Sinatra discussing it with Sam. Within a couple of months Sam had borrowed a large sum from Mickey, within a few weeks Mickey was leaning on Sam for payment, and within a few more weeks Sam was way behind in all his debts, including my salary. We would've parted friends, even though he owed me several hundred dollars, but he quibbled about the return of one of his old desk typewriters I had borrowed to start writing with Lenny, probably as an excuse to avoid paying my back salary.

During all this Lenny was impatient for me to start writing with him, and the Nick Lucas project with Frankie was dragging. I felt it should be a story about the recording and sound movie industry in which Nick was the first of a kind. Frankie felt it should be a story about a man, his family, his origins, and the countless little human episodes that made up his personal experience. It should have been possible for us to blend those approaches, but I think Frankie sensed I wanted to do something else and I'm sure I didn't hide it too well.

Between my bread-and-butter job and the increasing time Lenny demanded of me, I was finding it difficult to constantly revise drafts of the Lucas story, the unusual number of revisions partly an expression of the conflict between Frankie and me. Shortly after Frankie hired an Oriental woman to type the revisions, I "suggested" to Frankie that there was little else I could contribute to the project and I wouldn't feel bad about bowing out, leaving him to "collaborate" with the typist.

40

His reply was, "And I have a suggestion for you: go fuck yourself." And in one way I did. In the next ten years working with Lenny, I was never fully paid for a single thing I did.

Chapter 3
THE CREATIVE PROCESS

Comedy is as important as any form of art, literature, or media. As the leavening in the harsh reality of life, it is like those glands in our body that help us sustain shock and give us the time and the balance to reconnoiter our position and recoup for the battle. At best it does not deign to show us the battle plan for a brave new world, and at worst it does not become a garbage collector cataloging our refuse. Rather it helps us to see ourselves and our space, to live with the size and shape and color and gender of our mortal shell, and to evaluate the distance and conditions we place between ourselves and others, all through the eyes of a talented if not objective third observer, the comedian.

It is for the scientist to be objective. It is the talent of the comedian to show us how rubbery and flexible is the slide rule our peers use to measure us. If scientists can't get together on meters and inches, is it so surprising that some of us espouse equality, but think some are more equal than others, or that some champion objectivity, but think Satan's domain starts at the bedroom or bathroom door?

Satire, comedy's traditional raison d'etre, is the exaggeration of mannerisms until they are enough larger than life for us to recognize them in ourselves or our environment. When there is an excessive lethargy in a particular audience or about a particular subject, such as can be induced through a lifetime of conditioning by Madison Avenue or the church or the state, the degree of exaggeration needed to bring the subject to the audience's consciousness can approach the bizarre. Hence, Jonathan Swift's *Modest Proposal* and other milestones of satirical social comment through the ages.

I am one of the timorous crew who express their many and volatile differences with society through fantasy. When, at the age of eight, I took my first puff on a cigarette in order to blow smoke through a rubber tube and out of the mouth of my hand puppet, Clarence the Dragon, the resulting cough drew an unexpected laugh from the audience. Although I learned not to cough, I kept it in the act with the line, "It's bad enough I have to smoke, being a fire-breathing dragon and all, but you'd think that humans who didn't have to would have better sense." Hiding behind Clarence the Dragon, an eight-year-old could find the courage to disparage smoking, but the few times I have stepped out in front on much larger more serious issues I have frequently been verbally and physically abused or threatened.

I became an admirer and student of fantasy from *Gulliver's Travels* and *Alice in Wonderland* through a variety of religious texts to Jules Verne and *Star Trek*, for I believe the vast majority of fantasy I've read to be an effort to tell important and sometimes prophetic truths which society is too biased or apathetic to accept in any other fashion. I saw in Lenny the potential of a braver satirist than I could ever hope to be, a man who did not have to hide behind a puppet or a typewriter to state his opinion, but a man who could not focus his expression of that opinion into a marketable commodity that would reach a wider audience. I did not presume that I could manipulate Lenny like Clarence the Dragon to voice my many contentions with society, for Lenny was his own man and his humor was his own unique way of looking at the world, almost every bit of material a gem of purest satire looking for a whole entity to step into. It was that whole entity, a completeness which escaped Lenny each time inspiration sparked him, and he'd start at a climax and end with a fizzle.

That was to be my contribution: continuity, format, and discipline. It was my forte, and what I had contributed in my collaboration with Frankie. Constructing, pacing, timing, and, maybe once in a rare while, I could slip in my own personal zingers.

The first project was a comedy record, which up until this time was largely the domain of 'party records,' adventures in smut the more creative of which were pioneered by men like Redd Foxx, who slipped in many a succinct civil rights retort long before it became the vogue. Lenny had already performed on a comedy album as one of several comedians compiled on the Fantasy label titled *Interviews of Our Times*, with neither his name nor picture appearing on the cover. Years after his success they reissued the album, still without his picture, but with the words "Lenny Bruce''s" superimposed over the original title and photo, even though the contents were still a potpourri of different artists.

They liked him, they wanted to press him, but all they could find worthy in his act at that time were the few small bits they had culled for that first album. While two of those routines, *The Lawrence Welk Interview* and *The March of High Fidelity*, showed his preoccupation with the world of the jazz musician, the other routines showed the influence of Frankie's predilection for movie themes and talent as a dialect coach.

I convinced Lenny we had to provide a comedy script to offer Fantasy in order for them to invest in his solo album. I thought this would present no great challenge because I understood Lenny had previously scripted a film for Paramount called *The Rocket Man,* starring Charles Coburn, and another entitled *Dance Hall Racket,* which starred Lenny and his wife Honey. I learned later that Lenny had 'contributed' to the making of *The Rocket Man* through the sponsorship of a Paramount executive who befriended him and, when the executive died during production, Lenny's involvement ceased.

After seeing *Dance Hall Racket,* which only got into distribution years after Lenny died and was considered so bad it was 'camp,' I suspect there never was a script and the accusation I heard was true that it was largely a scam to get money from a backer who was primarily interested in scoring with girls in the cast.

Suffice it to say it was a chore to get Lenny to work at writing or accept some of the concessions that must be made to construct a piece for its overall good. But, in the end. Lenny was willing and appreciative and showed up regularly to write two to four hours a day, forsaking Joe Maini and the girls and bringing corned beef sandwiches or a bucket of chicken or chicken livers.

The latter was a warm and generous habit of Lenny's, particularly appreciated after I left Sam and went through a succession of jobs from tending bar at Barney's Beanery on Santa Monica Boulevard to selling motion picture equipment at Lloyd's Camera Exchange on Cahuenga. I finally decided to cash in my GI benefits to the tune of $110 a month for being a full-time student at Los Angeles City College. While tending bar at Barney's, I had to give up my apartment because they locked the front door at eight o'clock, and Lenny, in his zeal to help me keep my job by getting me there at nine, would stand outside the front door and scream my name until the landlord woke me up.

I got a studio apartment on Western near Santa Monica Boulevard, the other studios housing a tailor, a vocal coach, a Chinese laundry, and, coincidentally, an orthopedic shoe shop owned and operated by Lenny's father, who Lenny would avoid at all costs, including climbing over the rear fence to reach my studio during shop hours.

Barney's didn't pay much and the crowd was varied enough that you occasionally had to be a bouncer, but the food was good, the girls were plentiful, and it was fun seeing celebrities dropping in to enjoy the atmosphere and thank Barney for feeding them for free during their lean years. I saw a lot of Jonathan Winters, who didn't associate much with the crowd at Canter's; Walt Disney, who benefited from Barney's largess dating back to Disney's earliest beginnings; Walter Pidgeon, whose nephew tended bar in the bowling alley next door; Cesar Romero, with whom I had fascinating conversations, and many others on the town, on the bottle, or on the make.

Barney was a tall, tight-lipped, balding man in his sixties who peered through thick-lensed glasses as though he was always anticipating trouble. He probably knew more about the skeletons in Hollywood's closets than any other barkeep in town. His sister, whom I knew as a wizened, white-haired little old lady who worked in the kitchen like a galley slave, was reputed to have formerly been a famous and successful criminal lawyer from San Francisco. I enjoyed working there, but after a few months, Barney's adopted son was paroled from prison and needed a job, and it was tap city for me again.

While it is true that hunger and deprivation can be a fruitful environment for creativity, it's not the only environment for it, and it usually fosters far worse than creativity, but given the rare combination of certain other elements, it can be a chalice for inspiration.

I was raised in the midst of the Depression and knew hunger, not for a day or week or month, but for years. I know what it's like to hear your mother cry for want of being able to do anything about it. I know what it's like to be derided by middle-class children for wearing their hand-me-downs. But I also know what it's like to go to work when you're eight because you know something has to be done about it, to buy a piano when you're eleven with money you've earned, and buy a press camera when you're thirteen because there was a need in the community you wanted to see this instrument fulfill. In short, I know that what seems impossible can be done and dreams can be fulfilled, and deprivation can be a springboard to inspiration.

I remember picking up my last paycheck from Barney's and paying every last cent of it to my landlord, fearful of ever being in debt, never willing to finance anything through credit. On my walk home my stomach gurgled in response to the aromas drifting from the restaurants on Western Avenue. I saw a woman exit her car and enter a store, leaving her purse on the car seat. I held my breath so I couldn't smell the restaurants, and calculated in my mind the mathematical odds of being caught stealing the purse, how much there might be in it, how many meals it would buy in these restaurants, and how much dues I might have to pay if I were caught, by which time I was a half block past the car and had to resume breathing. After all, I was twenty-four years old and had been working the better part of sixteen of those years, and I'd be working again. I had been hungry before and I'd be hungry again. No big deal. I wondered if Lenny would bring some food that night.

When Lenny showed up with a bunch of those little square white cartons of Chinese food, I wouldn't eat anything until after we'd finished writing. I wanted to save the pain and passion of my hunger for those corrupt politicians, those hypocritical clergy, those thieving greedheads who had upset the balance of things and earned our scorn.

The first routine we scripted was *Religions Incorporated*. It grew from the seed of a throwaway line Lenny had, "You know the pope is Jewish?" based on the fact that the pontiff at that time had a huge proboscis. It always seemed to get a laugh and Lenny would throw it in anywhere there was the thinnest reference to Catholicism, Italians, Jews, or religion in general.

Lenny was fascinated that religion was the ultimate taboo to many people, despite the fact that its history was as filled with corruption as that of any other power in society. It intrigued him that Rocky, who had committed or condoned every last thing ever cataloged as a sin, would remonstrate him and become fearful of divine retribution every time Lenny used the line about the pope.

Lenny had worked in Miami and driven hastily across the south and west to reach California, but he knew little about the land of Dixie, its Protestant diversity, or its predominantly poor population, white or black. I shared some of my experiences and education on the subject with him, the factors leading up to the Civil War, the tyranny of the carpetbaggers, and the origins of the Ku Klux Klan. I told him of the ethnic diversity of Louisiana, the populist implications of the Huey P. Long regime, and the measures that kept the deep south a "house divided against itself." I illustrated the rural south I had known while working as a 'kidnapper' (baby photographer) shooting family pictures of children with rickets and malnutrition in dirt-floored schools and churches where ministers held up live snakes (blue runners usually, a long, iridescent, black, non-venomous chicken snake) in each hand as theatrical props to exhort a congregation eager to find expression for their economic plight.

These sessions became grist for many routines and later albums such as *Elect Me, I'm Not A Nut* (which was the pathetic platform of the then current Louisiana Governor Earl Longs re-election in the face of being institutionalized). They helped us delineate the characterizations of highly successful Protestant leaders who, for the same self- seeking and economic reasons as the equally corrupt politicians, helped foster ignorance and bigotry to keep a poor white and a poor black citizenry at each other's throats while they bilked the land's resources dry.

We had a lot of statements to make, a lot of villains with which to people our routines, but what we needed was a situation to place them in. I thought of a line from a poem by Pansy Benoit, a friend of my mother's. Pansy was a good woman, one of those poor white southerners who lived in the small town I was raised in. Pansy was dear to me and died of a heart attack on our front porch in a blackout (it was a mock night-time air raid drill) during World War II. Her simple poems were so like her and such a delight. This one was about her problems in finding affordable housing during those war years.

> *What in the heck has the world come to,*
> *There ain't a damn thing a poor fella can do,*
> *You can't find a house nor a shack nor a shed,*
> *But there ain't no use to shoot yourself dead,*
> *'Cause you'd feel outt'a place where the angels*
>   *dwell,*
> *And the politicians need all the space in hell.*

I borrowed Pansy's image of politicians creating a housing shortage in hell and suggested switching it to clergymen who didn't qualify for heaven going through all kinds of Machiavellian maneuvers with St. Peter to get through the pearly gates. We kicked this around for a long time, but finally shelved it, and it ended up being revised in a routine called *Show Business Heaven*, where a line we first attributed to a politician was eventually played against Lenny as an overpaid entertainer trying to get into heaven, "I've been saving some of mine [excessive salary] to give back."

Lenny didn't read much in the beginning, at least I never saw him read anything but the trades. Later he would give himself a crash course in law in order to effect his own defense in court. However, in those days he was always picking through my books and asking me about them. I had most of the works of Pearl Buck, John Steinbeck, Philip Wylie, Ayn Rand, and Vance Packard, in dog-eared paperbacks from thrift stores. There were enough different works by each of these authors to pique his curiosity and, after I would give him a brief critique of each of their works, he would try to stereotype them, which bugged me no end. Pearl Buck was sexually repressed, John Steinbeck was a hawk, Philip Wylie was a faggot, Ayn Rand was a dyke, but Vance Packard stumped him, probably because all his works were nonfiction and there was no emotional handle to him. He kept going back to Vance Packard's *Hidden Persuaders* and making me go deeper into a critique of that work. When I used the term "Madison Avenue" for the umptieth time, his face lit up and his hands made a frame in mid-air wherein he imagined the setting for *Religions Incorporated*. He said, "That's it. They're all on Madison Avenue planning next year's religious hustle."

A throw-away bit by Will Jordan, that he was afraid to do anywhere but for a few of us at Canter's, was the premise of two more routines we wrote. Will had Jesus returning to earth today to a jaded and indifferent public who refused to take him seriously, finally resorting to a theatrical booking agent to help him announce his coming, the agent modeled after Billy Grey (who played the theatrical agent in *Some Like It Hot* and other films). "So vot you need is you go get zum 8 x 10 glossies, go down to John Reed's, drop by Cy deVore's on de vey, he'll give you mebbe a liddle pinstripe mit der blazer, not too vide, den maybe ve give you a new name, Irish is in dis year, mebbe a nose job vouldn't hoit, a liddle bit toined up here." It was brief, nebulous, and too controversial for public performance at that time.

With all due respect to Will Jordan, for the first routine we applied the premise to Hitler with two Billy Grey types at MCA ("Mein Campf Arises") auditioning for

51

a new dictator ("Der Kaiser is oudt, he's had- dit") and discovering Adolf painting the walls. For the second, after the success of *Religions Incorporated*, we returned to Will's bit of Jesus's return and, without touching Will's lines, carried the fantasy one step further with Bishop Sheen and Cardinal Spellman as the jaded audience of the next coming. "Are you sure?" "Of course I'm sure." "Where is he?" "The one in the back." "Which one?" "The one that's glowing."

Some routines were lifted almost directly from life such as *Chicken*, wherein the pros and cons of being honest with your mate about sexual infidelities are analyzed. "Some guys will do it with anything. On a desert island guys will do it to mud. Some guys have even done it with a chicken." He was fascinated by this piece of sexual trivia I uncovered while researching antiquated sex laws for an article I was writing. Lenny couldn't get his mind off the ludicrous image of copulating with a chicken. "Whatever you do, don't ever confess. Say she came home and caught you with a chicken." Both Lenny's and Frankie's real life relations with women were grist for this routine, which perhaps touched the broadest segment in most audiences.

In my responsibility for 'rounding out the package,' I photographed the album cover based on the theme the Slate Brothers incident had stuck us with, *The Sick Comedy of Lenny Bruce*. Rejecting my ideas of having Lenny cooking hot dogs between his fingers while getting zapped in an electric chair, or having Frankie as a Roman soldier tickling Lenny as Jesus on the cross with a feather duster, mostly because the props were too costly, Lenny decided on the more tasteful and economical cover we ultimately shot of his eating a picnic in a cemetery. For the shoot, the only thing he told me was he'd made arrangements to use a setting in a major downtown cemetery, the one where Valentino is buried. But, as we drove in, he simply asked for a common name he knew there would be many of and, once through the gates, picked out a remote comer where he spread the picnic over a grave site, tried to look casual before the camera, and urged me to hurry up. I shot a dozen frames before a caretaker spotted us and started yelling, then charged toward us with shovel in hand. Lenny scooped up the picnic makings, I grabbed my equipment, and we barely made it to Lenny's old 1947 Chrysler business coupe with its elongated trunk before the caretaker arrived to eat our dust.

Lenny, however, could not perform the script in the studio. He needed the feel and response of an audience to give verve to his performance, but, to complicate matters for recording his live nightclub performance, he could neither remember a script nor did he want to do a routine the same way twice. Consequently, the live recording of a single routine had to be edited together from different performances recorded on different nights, on different equipment, and sometimes even in different nightclubs or cities. That's why they have such vastly different levels and tonality within some of the routines.

Scripting the routines had several benefits, though. For one, it helped sell the idea that Lenny Bruce could do a complete solo comedy album. Second, it proved to Lenny that he could do more than just bits, that he could build and pace a routine to a 'socko ending,' and that the resounding applause it produced, rather than the confused titter of earlier audiences used to hearing him leave unfinished bits hanging in the air, was worth the effort. And, finally, it produced a wealth of spinoff material, originally shelved and eventually dusted off, to become the basis of future routines, even after we no longer wrote together in a disciplined fashion.

Actually, our original script for the first solo album, *The Sick Humor of Lenny Bruce*, was not pressed in its entirety. Two of the routines, *Religions Incorporated* and *Hitler and the MCA*, were used, one on each side, and the balance of the record was filled out with more topical routines based on headlines of the day. Those headlines, about a man who blew up a plane full of people up just to collect his mother's insurance, a kid who fell in a well, and scandals of the Eisenhower administration, were not as universal nor as timeless as the original two routines.

Over a year later, a second Fantasy album, *I Am Not A Nut: Elect Me*, would employ two more of the original routines, *The Tribunal* and *Our Governors*, both edited somewhat from their original versions. While those two routines were both born of my personal experiences and, in their original form, had been co-authored by me, most of the first side of that album reverted to Lenny's habit of throwing out unstructured bits that gave promise of going somewhere, but arrived nowhere.

The smaller routines from the original album script were, none the less, complete routines and continued to appear in later albums right up to the last one we collaborated on before he died, which included the *Chicken* routine along with other things we had written together.

That's some idea of part of the creative process we employed. No one thing happens in one time. You force yourself to go in one direction until you find a fork in the road, make a choice, find you have to backtrack, and ultimately discover that, though the course to your principal goal is a crooked one, all those other roads do lead to some kind of a Rome; a Rome by any other name.

Chapter 4
THE FEEDBACK SYNDROME

Three people were critical to the turning point in Lenny's career. Most of all was Sally, his mother, whose contributions throughout his life were detailed in the autobiography I helped him write. Secondly, Frankie, his closest and most talented professional friend, was the first to recognize him as anything but a freaky novelty and the only one to offer him sustained moral support and professional tutoring throughout his career. And lastly, I merely carried Frankie's contribution one step further in terms of packaging, refining, and disciplining Lenny at a time when it was sink or swim in his career.

He might or might not have made the same impact on society without us. However, it so happens he made it because of our support and help and I believe understanding what we contributed is essential to understanding what he had to offer or what any prophet has to offer in his era.

Each of us is the sum total of our individual experience. What Lenny was, the good and the bad, was contributed to by a number of people in varying degrees of contact with him throughout his life. Most obvious to me was that his wife, Honey, and his most intimate friend, Joe Maini, were the most long-standing and integral influences in his personal life, and both were disastrous for his career after his initial success. Yet Lenny would not have been the person Frankie and I met in 1956 if he had not known Honey and Joe.

There are numerous people who aided and abetted Lenny after his initial success, most of them cataloged and quoted in other books about Lenny. I won't attempt to name them nor evaluate their contributions here. It would be dangerous and unfair to try to separate those who were sincere and valid from the many parasites that surrounded his success. Suffice it to say, I doubt that most of them would have found their way to Duffy's in 1956 or made an effort to lift the rough diamond of Lenny's talent out of that toilet.

There is a sea of professionals whose ideas and material flow back and forth in varying degrees from mutual collaboration to outright plagiarism. We all borrow, directly or indirectly, consciously or unconsciously, the more literally direct and conscious it is, the guiltier we may be of theft. The more indirect and unconscious, the more we delude ourselves that we have created original wisdom, but wisdom has always been there before us waiting to be discovered and built upon.

This feedback among entertainers was epitomized by Frankie Ray. He was fascinated by the construction of each individual character while I was fascinated by the larger construction in which the character was a component. We each needed and learned from each other, and many others learned from Frankie, including Lenny.

A short, dark man of Calabrian descent, Frankie's most noticeable trademarks are dark bushy eyebrows that make the baby face beneath them look all the smaller, the overall effect somewhere between Enrico Caruso and Leo Gorcey. His childhood education in Chicago consisted of constantly skipping school and seeing thousands of movies day after day.

Most children today experience a similar media glut in terms of the volume of their television viewing, but the commercials, the size of the screen, and the distractions and competing stimuli in the environment condition them to have a short-lived span of attention. I blame this in part for the inability of most of them to get anything out of the rare good programming available and their inability to sustain interest in any long range program in education or life. You can spot the TV raised young adult as the father who talks to his wife and throws popcorn at his children throughout the movie, the girl who fidgets in her seat and starts looking to see who's in the audience at a play, or the kid on the news who jumps off the rooftop to fly like Superman or accidentally shoots his buddies to death with his father's loaded revolver.

In Frankie's youth, and mine, the movie screen was the only available mass medium that could so completely capsulize an experience, a lifetime, or an era into two uninterrupted hours with all possible distractions submerged in the sea of darkness around you. You could concentrate on every dimple in Dietrich's anatomy, every whisker in Monty Woolley's beard, and every detail of the complex interplay they were involved in. Guns and gore and screeching car chases were not necessary if you could appreciate George Sanders's perfumed sneer, Mae West's tempting leer, and Claude Rains's tiny frame becoming a satanic giant on the screen.

Frankie went into show business very young and by the time he met me, and later Lenny, he had met or worked with most of those who had populated the movies of his childhood, saw them in three dimensions, watched them walk and talk and eat a hot dog at a drugstore counter. And he could recreate them, in walk, in talk, and in all those subtle dimensions that only the opportunity of firsthand knowledge could provide, and that the gift of Frankie's talent could perceive and reconstruct.

Frankie was more than a dialectician; he was a skilled mimic, and a large part of his own nightclub act was built around that particular talent. He was the first I ever saw to recreate a classic movie situation doing all the different characters himself. It was truly unique, but it was limited to a literal recreation and Frankie played it for the perfection of his impersonations, deviating from the original movie scene only to end it with something as comedic and incongruous as the hero stepping out of character far enough to tell his love interest to "bug off."

Frankie tutored Lenny in many things, particularly impersonations, and Lenny took Frankie's premise of movie situations, Frankie helping him perfect each of the characters, and improved upon the material by having the characters continually slipping out of character until the whole thing was a totally new and funny fantasy, the only semblance to the original being the plot.

Frankie had once did a double with Shecky Greene. He evolved into Shecky's business partner in a number of enterprises, was for many years Shecky's principal writer, and, though Shecky might roll his eyes at the thought, his tutor in some areas. Here again, the 'feedback' principle among comedians came into play. Although Shecky's brand of comedy is different from Lenny's, a sort of liberalizing and reaching for more bizarre limits fed back through Frankie from Lenny until Shecky's later material and performance were noticeably more volatile, incisive, and contemporary.

Shecky is now more or less mature and secure, but in those days he suffered enormous insecurities and, in his suffering, made life for those around him very uncomfortable at times. He was compulsive about food, liquor, and gambling, and he vacillated between dictatorial pomposity and abject fear that he would be rejected by an audience or a bellboy. Gerry, his wife at the time, was a beautiful but dominant woman who played Frankie and me, and anyone else around, like pawns in doing head trips on Shecky.

At one point, Shecky had acquired a Beverly Hills office and Gerry, Frankie, and I were decorating it. Gerry had bought a huge old rococo hi-fi at an auction, but its ancient radio receiver and speakers were not functional nor repairable. Gerry wanted me to install a mirrored cellarette in it and I estimated the cost at about fifty bucks. As an afterthought, Shecky wanted a new radio put into it so he could "listen to the races." When we went to dine nearby at Frescatti's, Shecky left early for a performance, after which Gerry told me that the radio had to come out of the fifty bucks and she'd "be happier if it were a crystal set." I ended up having to put a fifteen-dollar radio that sounded terrible in this ornate piece of furniture, and Shecky was frustrated for a long time trying to hear races he'd bet thousands of dollars on.

Later Shecky and Gerry bought a lovely house in a posh district in the San Fernando Valley and we were all brought out to oooh and aaah over it. They had also just adopted an infant child. Gerry got in a fight with Shecky over some trivia and reduced him to tears in front of everyone, then compared him to the infant. On the ride back to town, I sat in stunned silence while Shecky cracked jokes. Finally, referring to me, Shecky said to Frankie in a near hysterical voice, "Why doesn't he laugh? What's the matter, does he hate me? Does he hate me 'cause I'm fat? Does he hate me 'cause I'm Jewish?" All the while Frankie kept trying to reassure Shecky that I didn't hate him, I could only shake my head negatively. The truth was, I was so filled with resentment against Gerry and compassion for Shecky that, if I had tried to speak, I would have cried.

I think in those days Shecky was a little jealous of Frankie's involvement with Lenny and me. I think Shecky needed Frankie's friendship and emotional support at times as much or more than his professional assistance. Although some old habits die hard, they have remained close friends throughout the years.

One of the most important applications of the feedback syndrome in formulating Lenny's comedic approach was, again through Frankie, Lord Buckley who inspired a religious empathy in his audience far greater than their clergymen did. Lenny and Lord Buckley both were in an infinitely small minority who dared at that time to mix the license of comedy with the profundity of spiritual philosophies.

Lord Buckley was a sincere and greatly talented crusader for love, truth, and honesty. Many feel he died a martyr to a cause, refusing to obtain the required 'police card' while doing a one-night engagement in New York City. All entertainers resented the police card policy in New York City which, at that time, charged them $100 a year to be mugged and fingerprinted as no other citizen or professional was required to be, except known offenders on probation. Lord Buckley remained in jail in hopes of contesting the issue, but died in that same jail of an alleged heart attack incurred under suspicious circumstances. Many entertainers tried to raise funds to have his case investigated, but practically all feel he died a martyr to police discrimination against entertainers.

At the other end of the professional spectrum, yet every bit a professional and far more constant and intimate an influence on Lenny, was Sally Marr, AKA Sally Kitchenburg, Lenny's mother, confidante, and court of last resort when all else failed, as often it did. An attractive lady in her late forties when I met her in 1957, she appeared younger and often behaved like a hyperactive teenager in her exuberance and love of life. At the time, she was dating Tony Vascera, an ex-pachuco in his twenties with a love for the glamor of Hollywood and a talent for getting into the thick of it. At the time, he was studying hairdressing (he was the prototype for Warren Beatty's role in *Shampoo)*, and in the latter part of his life he was a successful theatrical agent representing such personalities as Cheech and Chong. Tony truly loved and admired Sally, and, despite her better judgment, married her. Though the marriage was short lived, their close friendship lasted throughout life.

Sally had been a nightclub comic for years at a time

when there were practically no women in that end of the business. Women had to make it on radio, the movies, or television, coming up through the ranks as actresses, dancers, or singers. Nightclubs were considered too rough-and-tumble for them, but not for Sally. She could stand toe to toe with whatever came on stage. She could squelch a heckler better than most men, and she was a master of the put-down. In the fondest sense, she was 'one of the boys.'

To know Sally is to immediately see where Lenny got what I keep calling his glandular condition, his hyperactivity. The only one I've ever known more quixotic than Sally was Lenny himself, and she suffered the same liabilities of temperament that Lenny did, principally the inability to concentrate effectively on anyone facet of her talents or one direction in her career. During the years that I've known her, she's been dozens of things, including a nightclub comic, a movie character actress (remember when she propositioned Art Carney in the last scene of *Harry and Tonto),* a theatrical agent, operator of a school for strippers, and for a brief period she was a 'dance consultant' at a Beverly Hills Arthur Murray studio, where she sometimes functioned more like a madame for gigolos.

While she was at the dance studio during those first few years when we were all starving, she talked me into wooing some of these lonely mature, but well-heeled, damsels in order to con them into investing in our film projects. My first conquest which she engineered was the wife of 'the zircon king of Siam,' a petite, plump, fiftyish lady with too much makeup, too little brains, a thick New York accent, and an estranged husband who was reputed to be the world's largest zircon importer. 'Madame X' lived in an ultra-conservative ultra-expensive hotel-apartment on Rossmore together with her tall butch-looking dominating sister, who eyed me like I'd stepped in something on my way through the garden. Sister treated Madame X like a child, as well she should for the poor woman was hard pressed to discuss anything beyond who her husband was and the weather.

I racked my brains to think of somewhere I could take the lady where I wouldn't be seen by anyone I knew, finally deciding on Ollie Hammond's on Wilshire, as the address was respectable enough for her, but the locale was a businessman's haunt where show people wouldn't be seen dead. As luck would have it, a vaguely familiar face at the bar tried to get my attention as I rushed Madame X through to the darkest recesses of the back room. No sooner had our drinks been served in a booth almost entirely hidden by plastic palms, when I was approached by the tall man with the familiar face who turned out to be a buddy who did troop shows with me while serving in Korea five years before. He had come to the West Coast to teach a class in comedy at a local university and there was no putting off his need to recall and recount the shows we had written and performed. By the time the dimness in the booth could no longer hide the age of my companion and the dimness of her intellect, I finally got my long lost buddy to take my address, phone number, and a strong hint to get lost. He ended up coming to dozens of parties to entertain everyone with a detailed account of my squirming agony at being caught playing gigolo to the wife of the zircon king.

Not only did the sister outmaneuver my efforts to get Madame X to invest in anything, but I soon met another older woman student at the dance studio who made me lose all interest in the rest of them. She may have been pushing fifty, but she had the body of a teenager with a spirit to match, and sexual capacity and proclivities equal to my own. As luck would have it, she didn't own a dime. She felt so guilty about shooting down my career as a gigolo, she offered to fix me up with her wealthy sister when the sister got a divorce, but the sister ran away with one of the dance instructors who took all her money. As a consolation prize, my amorous dance student offered to fix me up with her daughter, who was my age, but the daughter ran off to New York with her employer. I figured being a gigolo just wasn't in the stars for me, so, much to Sally's dismay, I retired from that short lived career.

I suspect Sally was a madame in a previous incarnation as she was always bringing women to me, actresses or entertainers she met in the business or students from her school for strippers. They all needed pictures or publicity or some service they had been told they could woo out of me with their charms.

I remember one beautiful but innocent looking little blonde from Idaho who, in our first and last interview, explained in her little girl voice the specific quantity and quality of sexual acts she would barter for my services, apologizing that the immediate installment would be brief as her young husband and two babies were waiting outside in the car. I longed for her willowy childlike body, but passed as I felt helping corrupt her would harm my karma.

An equally young and beautiful blonde I didn't pass on, as she was already corrupted beyond my ability to influence one way or the other, was one of Sally's stripper students who was the epitome of narcissism. No matter how intimate she might be with you in private, in public no one was allowed to appear to escort her, lay a possessive hand on her, or even sit too close for fear of intimidating the adulation of her audience on or offstage. Anyone could approach her, praise her, even flirt with her, but don't get too close and scare the others off.

The first time Sally and I took her to Tijuana, we cautioned her that her platinum hair and almost albino, white body (much less its construction) would cause traffic jams. She welcomed the attention so much she asked us to walk on the other side of the street so we wouldn't detract from it. When she couldn't navigate the first block without being mauled, Sally joined her to beat them back with a stick for the rest of her promenade down the main drag.

The other pole of professionalism from the Idaho innocent and the nubile narcissist was a brunette named Carmen who was referred to me indirectly through some of Sally's girls. Carmen was far more shrewd than the vast majority of such girls. She didn't trade sex; she 'used' sex to rapidly establish an intimate friendship and the opportunity to explore all the exploitable facets of that friendship. The only thing she admitted 'trading' in the process was modeling services for the periodic magazine glamor photography I did. She got more than some professional pictures and my place to crash in when she first hit town. She also got newspaper and magazine publicity from the glamor layouts, and she was paraded in a few choicely chosen places with choice people such as at the Villa Capri. Within three months, she no longer needed to crash at my place, she got a supporting role and second-line credit in a film with Frank Sinatra, and her colleague in the film, Shirley MacLaine, won an Oscar for the female lead, making Carmen's first film a classic. Success does strange things, though. It wasn't strange that I never saw Carmen again, but it was rather strange that I never saw another film credit for her. I hope whatever happened was good, although it's been my observation in this business that it usually isn't.

Some of Sally's contacts were a little more adventurous than I'd care for. Once she asked me to transport Tony's sister, her boyfriend, and her baby to Tijuana so the nfant could spend an extended visit with relatives there. These periodic visits to Tijuana were also partly to procure reasonably priced barbiturates without prescription. I was scared to death of narcotics, but I was

64

inexperienced then, uneducated about drugs, and naive enough to not include bennies and dexies in that fear. That was before I lived long enough to see friends and strangers convulse and die from barbiturate withdrawal.

Arriving in Tijuana, we left the baby with relatives, purchased our pills, and I hid my small stash in the pocket of my custom-made boots which appeared to be dress shoes with the tops covered by pants cuffs. The other boot-top normally concealed a Baretta .25-caliber automatic pistol, but, fortunately in this case, the weapon was not in its customary snap pocket.

The couple wanted to nightclub a bit, so we made the rounds and, largely to entertain them, I made a royal ass of myself with the petite and often delicious little Mexican strippers on and offstage. We ended up breakfasting at sunrise in a non-touristy part of town where the couple got into such a loud domestic fight that I moved from the booth to the counter in embarrassment. I suddenly sensed something had happened when, not only their fighting, but all sound in the cafe ceased. As I turned my head to look, I found a pistol barrel pointed at my forehead. An unkempt looking Mexican national glared at me over the sight of a much worn once nickel-plated .32 caliber Smith and Wesson, while he held the girl tightly by the upper arm and announced in Spanish that he was 'Policia' and was taking all three of us to the hoosegow. As we were herded into a two door Chevy as old and faded as my own, we doubted that we were truly in the hands of the police and feared we were the victims of some kind of shakedown or worse.

We were surprised and relieved to actually arrive at the Tijuana jail where we were charged with possession of narcotics, as the 'plain clothes man' had observed the couple popping pills. A search revealed nothing, as they had missed my boot pocket, and she had flushed her stash down the toilet despite the continuous observation of the male police personnel who had searched her most uncivilly and delighted in her embarrassment.

Our biggest problem was the young boyfriend from Chicago who, in his indignation, refused to offer them a bribe until we translated the Spanish we overheard for him which, in effect, said, "When immigration gets here in the morning, they'll know we can't hold them. So, either get them out of sight or get what you can before then, even if it's only a piece of ass from the chick."

The boyfriend turned pale, and, three half tones higher than usual, mouthed the phrases we carefully prepared for him to the effect that, "We're expected in San Diego this morning and they'll worry if we're late, so please take the only twenty dollars we have left to cover any fine for disturbing the peace, and we'll get out of your way." They took it and we left.

All in all, Sally was a rare education, more than a friend and less than a lover, like a buddy you love and admire, but whose judgment you don't quite have one hundred percent confidence in. While other mothers might have found her 'buddy' relationship with her son Lenny radical, I think Lenny still thought of her as a conservative maternal type. He delighted in having Sally come to his bedroom on some innocent pretext before throwing back the covers to reveal a naked blonde in bed with him. Sally was never thrown more than a half a beat before rallying with, "Cover the shiksa up, Lenny. The poor thing is blushing right down to her tush."

But in his hour of need, Sally was a mother in the finest sense of the word. Whether he was right or wrong, whether she understood or agreed or not, she was loyal to a love that extended throughout his life, from beginning to end. Many mothers might claim that, but few are put to the test to prove that love as Sally was.

For Frankie and me, Sally would often be the beacon that led us back to Lenny when, at the stormiest heights of his career, we were separated in body and mind.

Chapter 5
MAKING MOVIES

I never felt sure about what I wanted to do in life until I started writing with Frankie in El Paso and decided the ultimate art form is making movies. However, I never had the chance to attempt film production until I started working with Lenny, who was in the same learning process himself and was willing to do it on a shoestring, if necessary, in order to learn how.

Through the years I worked in three of Hollywood's largest cinema suppliers: Lloyd's Camera, Bob Gamble's, and Birns and Sawyer. I met most of the cinematic greats there from Hal Mohr, longtime president of the American Society of Cinematographers, right down through ASC's roster. I sold them the latest cinema equipment, checked them out on its use, and solved their problems when they returned. They were practically all good, talented human beings, but they were also all in their fifties, sixties, and seventies, and their advice and assistance to a young man trying to get into the business was, consciously or unconsciously on their part, little more than a total rejection. It took little research to realize cinematography was a closed shop rife with nepotism, as were so many aspects of the business. Lloyd Berman told me that, after he had come to Hollywood with similar ambitions, he had operated his store for fifteen years before he was offered a crack in the door as a 'camera loader,' lowest man on a five-man crew. By then he was in his forties, successful in business, and he told them to shove it.

Most of the advice from those inside had nothing to do with ability.

There were no schools for the industry then, and even classes available now offer little more than professional contacts. Most advice centered around how to 'join the club;' join this Turkish bath where influential gays hung out, join that temple where influential straights hung out, join an influential family by marrying the daughter.

Perhaps it is my fault that I could not pay those dues. I thought that valid dues were to learn my craft well if only I could find the opportunity. Lenny provided that initial opportunity.

After scripting the first comedy album and getting a commitment from Fantasy Records to record it, Lenny and I started on the first of three feature fiction scripts we were to write in those early years: *The Leather Jacket,* about a Chaplinesque character who attempts to compensate for his insecurities by acquiring a leather jacket and affecting a macho motorcyclist's image; *Killer's Grave,* about a bigoted Southern father whose attempts to hide the crimes of his mentally retarded adolescent son lead him to murder an old Jewish stonecutter at the local graveyard and ultimately his just deserts at the hands of an honest Southern sheriff; and *The Degenerate,* about a self-made evangelical preacher who is a lecher, a sadist, and a murderer in the course of contradicting everything he preaches. All three of these scripts were designed to be vehicles for Lenny in the lead role as anti-hero.

The Leather Jacket was chosen as the first vehicle because we felt it could be designed for a sufficiently limited budget to allow us to produce it ourselves and act as a springboard for the others. It was designed as a non-lip-synch art film with little or no dialogue, a budgetary consideration which also had some aesthetic validity. This approach gave the film more of the flavor of an 'art film.' It also gave Lenny a vehicle relying on sight gags and dramatic acting which would belie his growing reputation as a 'dirty-mouthed' comic. The first to propose the non-dialogue format was Frankie, who so loved similar techniques in Fellini films.

The Leather Jacket was a contemporary story which we adapted to the technique of the silent era. We took care not to lift any silent actor's piece of business totally, but rather discern the principle on which it operated and apply it. Lenny would become particularly sensitive when, during the writing and later during the shooting, I would draw these parallels and try to change the piece into our own distinctive creation. Lenny grew to resent the character being called 'Chaplinesque,,' even though the gestures and posturing which accompanied his complaint were the closest thing to Chaplin I'd seen in real life.

There was a silent movie house on Fairfax in Hollywood run at the time by a couple for whom it was a labor of love, researching, reviving, and reprinting many of the milestone films of the industry which no studio had the appreciation or foresight to do. I had been a devotee of the theater since my arrival in Hollywood and considered it then and now my finest schooling in cinema. The theater was poorly attended and the films mostly accompanied by appropriate recordings of old time piano music. If you knew your cinema history, you might recognize past stars seated in the audience watching their youth pass by on the screen, or shedding silent tears for departed friends who smiled through the projector's flickering light.

If you had a taste for the bizarre, there were a few probably harmless but seemingly deranged characters who would come in wearing long coats which opened to reveal period clothes and silent movie makeup mimicking silent stars. A few were men who would ape the effeminate gestures of particular silent male stars, mince over to a few seats from you, and silently mouth obscene overtures. But the cinematic lessons to be learned there were well worth the discomfit of the hard backed seats, the infrequent mishaps with the projector, and the occasional freaky friend.

During the writing of *The Leather Jacket,* I have no doubt Lenny was spending considerable time getting Frankie's input, as many of the ideas and sight gags Lenny contributed were flavored with Frankie's brand of humor with which I was so familiar. Frankie's huff over my leaving the Lucas project only lasted a few months and, when we commenced production on *The Leather Jacket,* he coolly began working beside me as a production assistant.

After finishing the script, I created a beautiful package with gold embossed leatherette hard binding for the script, which was typed on an IBM Executive typewriter. Bound in appropriate places in the script were photographic pages with creatively masked stills of Lenny and the cast from various key scenes in the film. Typically, we made three packages: one for him, one for me, and one for distribution.

My adventures with Lenny often centered around graveyards. For the stills in this script we went to a pet cemetery as one of the sites depicted in the script. The scenes and sight gags we shot there appeared almost identically in a Jonathan Winters' film some years later titled *The Loved One,* wherein one of the two characters Winters plays has many of the characteristics of our lead in *The Leather Jacket* and does the same action in front of the same little headstones appearing in our stills. In our film the site is one of several places our hero tries unsuccessfully to hold onto a job.

Without sufficient backing to start a 35-mm feature production, we decided to shoot a fifteen-minute pilot in 16mm black and white to establish the character and show together with the script at a backer's presentation.

I had been doing glamor photography with some of the dancers at the Near and Far, including a beautiful redhead named Jean Hidey who worked under the name 'Venus the Body.' Jean's husband, Hal Hidey, was a musical arranger for the Spike Jones Show and a vocal coach for leading vocalists. Jean was interested in photography and later became a professional glamor photographer herself under my tutelage. With Lenny's approval, I cast Jean as the love interest in *The Leather Jacket,* the sweet and compassionate streetwalker our pathetic hero falls in love with, but he doesn't realize she's a hooker and he can't take advantage of the opportunity she provides because society has emasculated him. Jean more than fulfilled the role's dynamic requirements. A natural actress and beautiful woman who exuded empathy and compassion, she had been taking camera direction from me for months prior and came across beautifully on film.

The first day we shot was the first time Frankie had talked to me in months and the first time I ever had a movie camera in my hands. I had borrowed John Neris' 16-mm Bolex with which he had made professional travel and anthropological films. Although John briefed me thoroughly on it and I was applying ten years of still photography experience to it, I still felt a little strained to actually put to the test all we had committed to paper, especially in front of Frankie who I was sure felt we should be embarking on his film projects first.

But Frankie was a real pro. Lenny gave me free rein, and Jean responded to the camera's every need. We shot on an abandoned side street near Fairfax and Santa Monica which we barricaded with our cars; Frankie stood guard over them when he wasn't playing makeup man, camera grip, or lunch caterer.

We had no motor drive, zoom lens, dolly, nor any of the usual professional equipment we felt we could not afford, but I fashioned a wooden dolly on the spot with wheels stolen off a shopping cart, fully exploited every prime lens we had, and wound by hand one sequence that was longer than the camera's spring motor would allow, yet was essential to the script. At one point I removed the trunk lid of Lenny's old Chrysler salesman's coupe from its hinges and mounted myself and camera in the trunk for a moving shot the makeshift dolly could not perform. I was acutely aware of the budget and anguished over the infrequent second and third takes that were required, but was adamant that my first effort was going to be done to the best of my ability.

My efforts were rewarded with everyone's ecstatic approval of the rushes, which fulfilled my fondest expectations and, I suspect, exceeded theirs. Lenny's exuberant approval of my cinematography insured my continued opportunity to learn not just cinematography, but the practicality of much cinema theory with which we had toyed on paper. We shot sporadically for several weeks whenever Lenny had the money for film and processing, borrowing or renting such a variety of cameras and equipment that I soon became acquainted with every 16 mm camera made at that time.

One day we were shooting at Melrose and Vine where a little triangular park in front of a church offered a larger than lifesize statue of Jesus for our woebegone hero to rest beneath. The compassionate expression and outstretched arms of the statue wordlessly amplified the exhaustion and frustration of our character in his flight from his failure to fulfill what he thinks society requires of him. The beautifully composed and sensitively played sequence makes a very positive spiritual statement as our hero, oblivious of the statue behind him is first disparaged by a hypocritical adult couple who see his shabbiness as an insult to the deity and their personal religion, then held in awe by a child from whose perspective the statue is relating directly to our hero, all the more so because of his shabbiness.

As we were about to do our third shot, a clergyman in full regalia came storming at us from the church, his robes flying in the wind and his Anglo Saxon face flushing redder every second. He disparaged us as "movie people," which we found rather flattering, "beatniks," although Lenny was the only unkempt one among us (being in costume), and "Jews," which was one of many times I unintentionally passed. He was not the least interested in what we were doing or why we had chosen to include his statue in our story. When we tried to explain, he then took the attitude of our make-believe couple and found Lenny's attire insulting to his religion and his person.

Finally, Lenny took a very Hollywood attitude and began a line of pure bullshit to the effect that it was a regrettable mistake that "Mr. Steinberg from accounting" hadn't contacted him first, as we had presumed, and if he'd call this number in the morning "the accounting department," which was supposed to have made arrangements for this location, would have a check out to him posthaste which would cover the day's shooting and a hundred dollars a day for any additional days needed.

The clergyman, who had no further evidence that we weren't really making an atheistic propaganda film for the communists, was more than mollified, he was apologetic, willing to let us finish shooting, and we were welcome to use the telephone and the john in the church if needed. When the clergyman called Lenny's home phone the next day, thinking he was reaching "the accounting department," Lenny pretended to be a stranger who thought the priest was trying to rent him the statue for unnatural acts at $100 a day and countered with an offer to pay the asked for price for an attractive nun by the night, "But she has to be in habit."

We were stymied for want of adequate studio space to shoot the dream sequence, which was to be in color and the sexiest part of the film. It would be shot in two versions with Jean partially nude in one and totally nude in the 'European release' form. Finally, through the sale of some of my magazine photography, I was able to afford a larger studio at 7511 Melrose, and, after putting in a darkroom and office partitions, we built the dream set in my new shooting room.

The building was only about fifteen feet wide despite its sixty-foot length. With the widest available lenses, we still couldn't shoot across the fifteen foot dimension and achieve the desired coverage, so we built the set in the fifteen-foot width in order to manipulate the camera in the longer dimension. To keep the side walls from showing in the 'sea of darkness' we desired, we had to paint the floor and walls flat black, which, months later, almost gave the landlord a heart attack. I called upon my years of working in little theaters in the south to design and construct a set out of discarded tubes that linoleum comes rolled on and seamless background paper. We fogged our set by dropping dry ice in off camera buckets of water at strategic moments during filming.

This was the first time we had enough money to rent a fully professional reflex camera, allowing me to actually see through the lens in order to manipulate the special effects in the camera. Lenny shared my enthusiasm as I reveled in the potentials it offered. I experimented with distortion filters; varying degrees of Vaseline smeared around the perimeter of a clear glass filter to provide a sharp center with soft edges; flashlight lenses with diamond pencil scratches around the perimeter to achieve specific flares; and window glass heated over the stove to achieve lateral ripple distortions, then cleaned and used in the camera's matte box.

The widest angle lens we could find for the Arriflex camera was a 16mm focal length, only moderately wide at best. In little theater productions, I had created projected backgrounds in short backstage throws by adding photographic diopters in front of the projection lens. With the reflex camera, I experimented with this technique to discover that a bizarre fisheye effect could be achieved with the non-photographic lens used in door peephole viewing devices. Mounting the little peephole lens in a metal lens cap in front of the 25-mm normal camera lens worked best and it produced the surrealistic effect we wanted to exaggerate parts of Jean's anatomy and parts of the motorcycle we used in the scene.

The bike was a trip and a half. For the stills incorporated in the script, we had gone to a biker's hangout on Cahuenga, got to know some of the gang, and included them in our stills. One particular guy had the most outrageous 'hog,' a Harley Davidson of monstrous proportions with everything ever manufactured as a tasteless accessory on it. It blinked, it beeped, it even sang Dixie, or at least the first two bars of it. He and his girl were happy to cast the bike in the film for a few bucks. We had to remove the front door to get the bike in and I had to devise a power supply for its extensive lighting system to keep the battery from dying in the middle of a take. The poor guy didn't know whether to be more concerned about how I mounted his bike on a black cloth-covered wooden jig and hooked into his light system, or the rest of my crew who ogled his tightly dungareed blonde girlfriend who was shockingly braless, an open invitation to lust in those days.

With Jean's long red hair, dancer's body, and classy choreography, the dream sequence came out beautifully. If the original 16mm footage had gotten into distributable form within a year or two of its creation, it would have made a very positive statement about our film making abilities. But it never did.

Lenny would not let me edit the film. He needed me in too many other areas and was spreading me thin, perhaps thinking I would leave him any moment for something better, although I had no such intentions. Our troubles began because he was attempting to edit the film himself and allowing any and everyone who said they were an editor to assist him or take over segments of the film. Both Lenny and some of these other unqualified people were not only wasting our time and money with cuts that had no merit or relation to our story, but worst of all, they were committing the unpardonable sin of cutting the original footage, sometimes with the excuse of economy in not buying customary work print, but with irreparable damage to our project.

The first inkling I had of this was when Lenny released a 45-rpm single with a parody song, *Psychopathia Sexualis*, on one side and a heavy death row recitation on the other. He had a chance to plug it on The Hank Weaver Show, a local TV talk show, and wanted me to shoot a promotional film for it with practically no money or time.

I did a quick storyboard, made pen and ink artwork in miniature cutouts, and shot the film in sequence, using a laborious stop-motion animation technique with in-camera dissolves and optical effects, to eliminate editing and minimize cost. Also, it was timed to the record by the tedious method of frame counting because we didn't have time to edit it double system. I finished it less than twenty-four hours before air time and tested it once, its broad overlapping segues giving it ample room to match the record in a wild non-synch playback.

Lenny was in a hyper state when he picked up the film, and accompanied by some of a growing collection of hangers-on, one of whom was an aspiring editor with no education other than the instruction book to a $25 home moviemaker's kit. Lenny and this 'editor' managed to hack up the little film so much that by air time it bore no relation whatsoever to the record. Lenny wanted to reward me by crediting the film to me, and I said, "Please don't."

He was miffed by my disapproval of his re-cut and carried my disclaimer over to exclude my credits when Hank Weaver queried him about *The Leather Jacket,* the album, and all the other work we were collaborating on.

This rift started towards the end of the first year we began working together, but did not tear us asunder until the end of the third year, 1959, when Lenny was at the height of his initial success. For a long time I did not know what was going on with the editing. For the most part, I was submerged in the day-to-day struggle to keep my studio and my head financially above water. I had taken a speculative contract from Lenny on the film and would see no returns until and unless the film succeeded. I had no contract for the writing or photography I did on the albums, and ultimately would never see payment for it.

Lenny paid the barest expenses and manipulated circumstances to keep me in his corner. If I was hungry, he brought food. If I needed materials to experiment on his projects, he bought them. At one point I was so strung out working for him that I hadn't had sex for a month nor funds to socially pursue the same. He paid a stripper to seduce me, knowing how loathe I was to accept commercial favors.

Despite the circumstances, I was elated at having my new studio and a small but growing number of advertising, magazine, and theatrical accounts which enabled me to expand my equipment and the scope and caliber of my work. I was disappointed when Lenny stalled me in fulfilling his promise to pose as Jesus on the cross now that I finally had a place to do the set in, but I found a variety of other satisfying things to do.

While I was moving into the studio, a small record company was moving into the adjacent building. They had a good package designed to sell to dance instructors and students. It consisted of original music for a dance routine recorded on one side of a 45-rpm disc and a practice version with vocal instruction of the same routine on the other side, packaged in a book-like jacket that included sheet music, costume design, and choreography both written and illustrated with step-by-step photographs. The idea would have succeeded if the promoter of the company hadn't sold 150% of the holdings and disappeared. For the first six months, however, I did their artwork and photography for which they paid promptly in the beginning, then became increasingly late until they finally beat me out of $800. Until then, I very much enjoyed the work and meeting a great variety of dancers, a group I've always had a fondness for, and some of whom I would work with years later in other media.

In between a few seemingly solid clients like the little record company, I did album covers, advertising photography, and, my favorite, glamor photography. This was the principal period during which Sally kept sending girls to me and, for every two or three cash clients, I had one with rounder, softer coins.

Initially, I took a partner into the studio, a dear friend who I met in the Air Force in Korea. Keith Hemphill's goodness, honesty, and generosity more than made up for what he lacked in sophistication and tact. Originally a carpenter, he became a competent commercial photographer through Air Force training, producing all those aerial photographs I had to critique in Korea, but he was not into my kind of photography and, after four months, I bought his interest in the studio. In the beginning, though, we shared the adventures of being poor and trying to start a business on a shoestring.

In economic desperation, I talked Al Warner, owner of the Near and Far, into letting me operate a piano bar in the club four hours prior to his normal opening time, splitting the net. We rented a spinet piano, built a formica bartop for it, and Keith was ensconced as apprentice bartender frequently coming over to whisper, "How do you

80

make a daiquiri?" in my ear as I played at the piano bar. We became acquainted with the garden variety housewife hookers who freelanced in the neighborhood and decorated our bar with their presence in exchange for free Seven-Up in a martini glass and the freedom to ply their amateur trade on our premises. The luridness of the burlesque house marquee was a bit too intimidating for a cocktail hour trade, but we struggled with the operation for a few months, deriving more nourishment from cocktail olives and cherries than any monetary proceeds.

Hunger again fed my dramatic sense and Lenny and I progressed to the appropriately dramatic *Killer's Grave.* This story, set in a small southern town, was most directly related to the growing exchange of experience between Lenny and me and his interest in my southern background. He was surprised to learn that many southerners, even some southern sheriffs, were not bigots and were even honest and fair. He was fascinated with the thought that most southern Jews did not speak with Myron Cohen accents and many, who might look very much like Lenny, had noticeable southern accents and flew little confederate flags from their auto antennas.

He was also titillated by the idea that many southerners found graveyards far from depressing, but rather peaceful, and even romantic. I showed him my autographed books by Robert Talent, a customer and friend from my French Quarter days, who wrote several nonfiction books on the subjects of voodoo and Marie Le Vau and a whole fiction series about *Mrs. Candy*, whose life among New Orleans's lower classes during the Depression was comically and compassionately mediated by her incessant graveyard consultations with her departed husband. Lenny found it hard to believe my description of headstones with tintype photographs framed under glass, some with exquisitely phrased and illuminated poetry engraved in rare marble, and some that at- tempted to unkindly and unfairly sum up a human life as an "illegitimate child," a "faithless wife," or a "murderer."

We pictured our story's setting as such a graveyard, and I originally hoped to shoot the film on location in the south, in order to capture the beauty and curiosities of the specific cemeteries I had known. Lenny, however, was always impatient to pursue the next project before the previous one was completed, and we began scouting Los Angeles cemeteries for such a location before either *The Leather Jacket* or *Killer's Grave* had been realistically funded. We found an appropriate location in a graveyard devoted to temporary interment of remains awaiting shipment overseas. The headstones had a foreign flavor, if not authentically southern, right down to the glass-framed photographs and occasional reference to the sins of the deceased. Using this cemetery as the principal location, we began to weave the nucleus of our story to fit the available site and existing props.

Like *The Leather Jacket,* this film's theme was one we felt would play well in black and white, and we began to structure it visually for this mood. I shot hundreds of black and white stills in the graveyard, picking out camera angles, establishing specific daytime hours for natural lighting effects, and cataloging details of the stonecutter's shed and tools we might have to reproduce on a sound stage. I made a map of the site and annotated 'no-play' areas where we could tie in inserts from other locales of features this site did not offer. I climbed up a water tower we would be shooting from, strapped a box with a concrete block in it to my shoulder to approximate the size and weight of an Arriflex 35mm camera, and, while Lenny lay across my legs as a counterweight, I practiced various intricate hand-held shots that would sometimes leave me hanging upside down from the water tower.

The final script was supposed to exploit all of this preplanning and was a very well designed low-budget film.

Then, it could have been shot in ten days at an overall cost of $35,000, including the going rate for a low-cost name like Lon Chaney, Jr. in the role of the sheriff and scale salaries for most of the cast and crew. Two years later Lenny would earn that much in less than a month, but at that time we didn't have any hope of financing it unless *The Leather Jacket* succeeded.

Lenny got some limited funding to start shooting *The Leather Jacket* in 35mm. I got Lloyd to rent us the equipment on speculation, and we started re-shooting much of the original pilot we had done in 16mm. We were still working in the Fairfax and Santa Monica Boulevard area, but with more equipment and cast and crew than we could afford when we had made the pilot. Soon we were making enough smoke to attract the union.

Two huge guys out of a Dick Tracy comic strip started to shadow us, then overtly harass us. Three seconds into a take they'd walk in front of the camera, and no number of volunteer 'guards' were able or willing to stop them. They'd do everything to try to damage or sabotage equipment and threaten or pick a fight with cast and crew.

At one point we were attempting a special effect where Lenny is asleep sitting on the ground with his back against a parked car, when the owner pushes him rudely aside and enters the car. Lenny's hand is accidentally caught in the door as he grips the jamb in an effort to rise. We shot the long shot in which his hand is not actually in the door jamb, but all action and reaction is performed in continuity. Then we set up the special effect insert by framing a closeup of the upper half of the door and excluding the lower half where an unseen 2 x 4 blocks the closure of the door, allowing 3 ½" for Lenny's hand to grip the door jamb safely even when it's slammed against the 2x4. From the camera's view- point, the first slam would appear to be on Lenny's hand, Lenny would remove his hand, I would deliver a verbal cue to a grip lying on the rear floor of the car to pull the 2 x 4, the second slam would close the door completely, and the car would drive off. We rehearsed the routine several times to perfect it.

During a take, everyone involved in it, in front of or behind the camera, is bound to be nervous. In addition to wanting a perfect take, there's money at stake in terms of a foot and a half of expended film every second that the camera hums plus the greater expense of everyone standing around whether participating at that moment or not, as well as myriad other contingencies that everyone, including the grip lying on the floor of the car, is nervous about.

As we started to film the insert, Lenny gritted his teeth and positioned his hand on the door jamb according to my instructions. The door was wide open, and we were supposed to see the car owner enter the car, glare at Lenny, apparently slam the door on Lenny's hand, Lenny remove his hand, the door slammed fully closed, and the car drive off.

The camera and the action started, the car owner entered the car, glared at Lenny, and started to slam the door for the first time when a strange voice boomed out the cue, "Pull!" The grip obediently pulled the 2 x 4 and, miraculously, Lenny pulled his hand out just before the door slammed completely shut.

We all looked around furiously at the source of the voice that delivered the dangerous cue to see the snaggle-toothed smile of one of the goons who had been harassing us. He pinpointed me as the youngest and most likely to reach the boiling point, so he began to sing-song at me, "Pull, pull, pull." I took the bait and, picking up part of a camera shoulder brace to use as a club, started to rise, but was restrained by the others. The goon, obviously feeling he had precipitated enough of an excuse to damage the equipment, pushed the camera over. I instinctively dropped my club and threw my arms around Lloyd's already battered old 35mm Arriflex, and we both went down, the camera safely on top and I painfully on the bottom. Seeing I was in a no-win position, I continued to lie on the ground clutching the camera until the goon left.

Lenny tried a dodge by getting Debbie Reynolds, then an official of the Thalian's theatrical organization, to sign us a waiver to shoot a non-union film on the streets ostensibly for an upcoming Thalian's project. Debbie Reynolds bought the ruse, but the union didn't.

Next Lenny took another circuitous route. In those days the National Association of Broadcast Engineers and Technicians (NABET) was almost exclusively a broadcast union with a few ill-defined applications to film production. Lenny got Bill Himes, then president of the NABET local, interested in the project and, giving him a piece of the film and giving him my position as Director of Cinematography, Bill Himes got the goons off our back simply by giving the NABET stamp to the project.

The association, however, created other conflicts in our production. Bill Himes was a technical perfectionist who could not abide our makeshift methods and equipment, which was more a result of budget than ignorance on our part, and Lenny ended up trying to make me Artistic Director over Bill's cinematography in order to retain the flavor we had incorporated in the script and pilot, as well as to keep me involved in the project. This infuriated Bill Himes in view of the disparity between our ages and years of experience. Thereafter, I tried to keep a low profile as far as he was concerned, and relayed my contribution directly to Lenny with suggestions as to how some things might be achieved without ruffling Bill's feathers. I learned a lot of things from observing Bill at work, but I also found a lot of it to be more by the book than most independent production has time or money for, and which can sometimes get in the way of achieving the spirit of the story line.

To stay out of Bill's way, I began to shift my duties from behind the camera to in front of it with Lenny's grateful approval. In one scene I played a homosexual who tries to pick up our hero at a bus stop. However, the hardest scene I played was the prologue, which was also the end of the film, where Lenny is brutally beaten by a motorcycle gang who misinterpret his fascination with their leader's leather jacket. As one of the gang, I am supposed to punch Lenny realistically. After two bad takes, Lenny started yelling at me, "Don't hold back, go ahead and do it for real. Hit me as hard as you can in the gut." I felt foolish that, with all the acting I had done, I couldn't convincingly fake a punch in this closeup. I didn't want to spoil another take so. on the next one, I let it fly, Lenny threw up all over me, and I felt miserable for hours afterwards about hurting him.

Unfortunately, Bill Himes tired of the meager budget, the shooting schedule, and Lenny's temperament. The final straw was when Lenny decided to go back to 16mm to finish the production. *The Immoral Mr. Teas* had just hit the market as the first 'sexploitation' film to successfully be shot in pin-registered 16mm and blown up for 35-mm distribution, a sort of milestone accomplishment in reducing initial budget costs. I agreed with Bill Himes that we couldn't adopt this approach for a number of technical reasons: we were dealing in black and white which had a grain problem unlike a color film; *The Immoral Mr. Teas* was shot on the finest grain slow film under optimum studio lighting conditions which we had not done nor could do; *Mr. Teas* was shot entirely with pin-registered cameras, which much of our previous footage was not; and, most of all, *Mr. Teas* was shot for a committed distribution and projection system and would be largely unsalable to the outside market we had to deal with.

But Lenny was grasping at straws to try to finish the film, both for the momentum it might afford his career and, to free him should the success of the record create a demand for his nightclub act to go on the road.

I agreed to continue with the project where Bill Himes left it, but it was terribly disorganized by then, much more than I realized or was allowed to know. To me, it was my first film, and I yearned to see it come to life before an audience. I could not believe it was destined to be stillborn.

Chapter 6
COFFEEHOUSE CAPER

Lenny and I began working together as the beatnik era reached its zenith and began to wane. I don't think Lenny had read Jack Kerouac's books, but he was very much a product and an integral part of that attitude. Though I do not recognize it as a philosophy as such, to me the beatniks seemed to plead for some alternative expression against a corrupt and hypocritical society, other than the beatnik's own self- destructive bathlessness, booze, and bad language. Lenny, though in part a victim of this confused thinking, was one of the few who sought and espoused a positive alternative expression to society's ills. He would not join the conspiracy of social hypocrisy and corruption, but at the same time he did not feel 'beat,' at least not in the beginning.

Coffeehouses, the meeting places of beatniks, were transplanted from New York City to Hollywood in the late fifties with the opening of the Unicorn Coffeehouse on Sunset Strip. The management included Herbie Cohen, a tall, lean bearded fellow named Rudy who later opened The International on Cosmo Street, which later moved around the comer to Cahuenga and became Shelly's Manne Hole in partnership with famous jazz drummer Shelly Manne; and Benny Shapiro, who was put in charge of the Unicorn Corporation's second venture, called Cosmo Alley. Benny was eventually squeezed out of the Unicorn Corporation and he opened The Renaissance on Sunset Strip.

I had become a devotee of the coffeehouses when I first arrived in Hollywood, making the rounds of them, in contrast to the posh restaurants I worked in with Sam Wall and the older atmosphere of Barney's Beanery. The coffeehouse crowd were more my peers than the people I worked with, who were one or two generations older. In the coffeehouses people played folk songs on a variety of stringed instruments for the fun of it, guys who didn't know you would invite you to play chess, and the girls were all in some kind of dance or yoga class and wore leotards under their gossamer wrap-around clothes.

I knew Benny Shapiro from the less than successful opening of Cosmo Alley and through Benny's later friendship with Lenny, which I suspect stemmed from the drug culture. I liked Benny and was active in his management of both Cosmo Alley and later the Renaissance, but on a social level we moved in different circles.

Benny was among a small but growing cult of people who hero worshiped Lenny. Many of them did not understand what Lenny was saying or doing, but because they so strongly identified with one or two of his barbs against society, they wanted to champion him as their avenging angel and pay homage to him in any way they thought would please him. One way was to show him they were in accord with his label of 'sick comedian,' which they tried to prove by out-grossing him.

Frankie threw a birthday party for Lenny one night at the Near and Far after hours. Most of the gifts reflected the cultist's idea of 'sick humor' from soiled Kotex to the most macabre, a bloody, dismembered baby doll in a box with a card signed "The Lindberghs." Lenny really wanted to denounce the humor, but he could not resist the adulation.

The cultists presented a problem to Frankie's and my efforts to keep Lenny focused on his career. They seduced his ego with their adulation, they sucked up his time and energies with their hospitality, and they exposed him to more drugs than his will power could handle. But, if Frankie or I tried to reason with him, we, if not Lenny, felt our criticism might be biased with envy, and it was an increasingly difficult task to discipline our work together.

Benny and I got along fine, however, and it was my acquaintance with him that led me to become involved in coffeehouse management and subsequently interesting Lenny in them, although it was a very circuitous route.

When I started attending Los Angeles City College, I quickly found I couldn't survive on the $110 a month provided by my GI Bill. I reluctantly decided to share an apartment in order to cut expenses and picked a middle-aged jazz music student named Gerald Murphy because, among the group of Westlake School of Music students with whom I was acquainted, he was the most mature and least volatile.

Westlake was one of those trade schools that sprang up during the postwar years to soak up the GI Bill money that was floating around among veterans who too often opted for something glamorous rather than practical. Although it was eventually audited out of business by the government who saw it as a parasite preying on veterans, Westlake created one of the few opportunities to organize and subsidize a serious study of jazz outside of the more pedantic university environment. Westlake and its alumni contributed noticeably to modern jazz in gen- eral and West Coast jazz in particular.

Many of the Westlake students I knew are stories unto themselves, but the group among whom I met Murph was by far the most colorful. They lived, some five to seven of them at a time, a block from the school in a courtyard cottage that looked like something out of a Disney movie with freeform shake-tile roof, asymmetrical leaded windows, and dense shade trees you expected the wicked queen from *Snow White* to peer around as she spied on the seven dwarfs from Westlake.

At any hour of the day or night you'd usually hear

one or more of them playing on a great variety of instruments. The place was eternally littered with handwritten music charts, dirty dishes, half-eaten junk food, and musical instrument cases which served as occasional tables amid a half-dozen mattresses dotting the floor, the only furnishings.

Paul George was the nominal head of this small band, largely because he was the only one with a rich dad to bail him out of dire emergencies, a tactic he was loathe to exercise. A handsome young Arabic version of Castro, Paul was softspoken and lovable, but, in his conflicts with his father, he had acquired many of the old man's worst traits from ruthless business ethics to playing head trips on others, as well as a passionate anti-Semitism.

Paul perceived my Jewish associates, Jewish expressions, and work in publicity and film production as evidence that I was Jewish, yet he was puzzled by his rapport with me, which did not compute with his father's philosophy. He was always looking for the hook, the sting, in everything I did, whether it was bringing care packages to the group at Disney Manor, organizing them into a working musical aggregation so they could get casual bookings, or bringing groceries periodically after his wife and two babies joined him. Ultimately, Paul sold out to his father's lifestyle, helped expand the St. George musical instrument empire to the West Coast, and alienated me along with many of his friends with an attitude of swaggering upsmanship.

Although very passive by nature, Gerald Murphy was the senior member of this group and, despite Paul George's more aggressive leadership when I first met them, they made certain deferences to Murph. He was counselor, mediator, and quasi-father figure to many of them. In his late thirties and looking like a balding Irish cop, he was at the crossroads of his life, having given up on a second childless marriage and seeking whatever it was he wanted to do with his life and for himself rather than always for someone else. Jazz music represented a great divergence from his former life and he found it very satisfying, even though at first he showed only nominal aptitude and talent. He later tried electronics and finally technical writing, two fields as equally challenging as jazz music to his growing inability to concentrate. At one point he thought he had narcolepsy and turned to barbiturates, only to become addicted to them. In later years he kicked the barbiturates only to succumb to alcohol, dying of its complications in his fifties.

Despite marking himself as a loser since before I ever met him, Murphy had many positive virtues. He was somewhat musically talented, he had even more literary talent, and he was most adept at satirical comedy in which his paranoid outlook on life could always find the most unlikely and bizarre banana peel for any hero to slip on. But, like so many talented people I've known, he couldn't concentrate and focus his talents; he couldn't "get it together." Whatever his failures resulting from manipulating himself into a self-fulfilling prophecy of being a loser, Murph succeeded in one thing few others do, he didn't manipulate others. This one success led many to sincerely respect and love him.

While Murph was ten years older than I, I in turn was two or three years older than most of the Westlake group. Murph welcomed the opportunity to room with someone more mature in character, particularly someone who had a piano, could coach him in keyboard harmony, and would collaborate in writing short stories and comedy.

Murph worked as a part-time guard for a Hollywood security firm that also operated a detective agency. We had both dabbled in electronics, he to understand and repair his guitar amplifier, I to understand and execute the audio needs of magnetic and optical film recording devices. When he learned that his employer's detectives were, in their electronic ignorance, having problems utilizing eavesdropping devices, he referred me to them as a specialist in the field. Actually, it was a short step from my applied experience in audio to the technology used in bugging, and when Murph suggested it to me as a part time income, I brushed up in a few days on the additional information needed.

The agency was owned and operated by an ex-FBI man named Frank Angel, who looked like a white-haired Dick Tracy. His main man was John Boyles, a round-faced, slightly heavy, red-headed Irishman who delighted in 'difficult' situations. The two were well known, if not notorious, in certain Hollywood circles during those days.

I auditioned for the job by making and surreptitiously installing a bug in Frank's office, using it to record an interesting conversation between Frank and John Boyles minutes before my scheduled interview, and playing the tape to his surprise during the interview, presenting the tape and concealed bug to him as a finale.

I was offered $5 an hour, $50 minimum per installation, no overtime increases, plus expenses. I was naive to accept, but this was the late fifties and that wasn't bad then for a freelance job you could accept or reject at your own discretion. I learned they were paying some guy in Florida $50 apiece for the commonly used miniature wireless bug, so I started manufacturing them at that price from $3 worth of parts encapsulated in epoxy in the little cubicles of a plastic ice cube tray. In one evening with little more than $50 worth of parts I could make $1,000 worth of bugs in a single tray, but Frank didn't use them fast enough to use up the first batch I made and I eventually used them in Lenny's house, which Lenny had me bug thoroughly during its construction.

Most of the jobs were routine installations for jealous spouses, insurance fraud, or industrial theft, and rarely exceeded the minimum payment. In short order I learned the rudiments from John Boyles. Always park your car pointed in the exit direction. Never park your car where it can be blocked. Always rehearse your cover story before you enter the grounds. Always carry workman's coveralls and visored cap to cover your streetclothes when needed. Unless licensed, carry a weapon only in a locked container such as briefcase, toolkit, or glove compartment, even if you have it illegally unlocked while working. Frank didn't want to license me through his office because of the questionable legality of my particular work, and I was not keen on having to produce the little .380 hammerless MAB that was always with me on the job.

One job which didn't require the MAB, but which would not normally have fallen to me because it didn't require electronic surveillance, was from the management of Cosmo Alley whose books indicated skimming somewhere in their cash flow. When I told Frank I knew the manager personally, he gave me the job. It turned out I was mistaken because, unbeknown to me, Benny Shapiro had been squeezed out of the Unicorn Corporation and a young man named Jack Sikking was now in charge and requested the investigation. Jack had previously managed the Purple Onion on Sunset Boulevard, helping make it a successful jazz nightclub, and had been hired to revamp Cosmo Alley's image from a profitless beatnik haunt into a similar success.

Class acts like Josh White, Odetta, and Theo Bikel, who himself bought a piece of the club, brought in a more mature and affluent clientele titillated by the remnants of the place's beatnik past which Jack accented with touches like gilding the exposed plumbing and painting the brickwork black and then scratching artistic cracks and scars to show brick-red through the black.

Jack was shrewd and talented at things, but not people. The staff were part of the decor to him, not people to be communicated with or developed for the good of the whole operation. The waitresses were hired for their looks; black, oriental, olive skinned, and blonde, decked out in custom-made elfin caps, shoes, and waistcoats over contrasting light colored leotards intended to show off their figures. Some were hired because they were relatives of famous jazz musicians such as Art Pepper's wife and Dave Brubeck's younger brother who tended bar.

All Jack's staging, his carefully placed dimmer controlled mini spots, his European design ceramic and wicker serving pieces, his beatnik-cum-Mandarin black and gold and red decor, and even his elfin sex symbols did not contribute one bit to any feeling of stability, security, or belonging, which he failed to give his staff. And of course, it was most of his staff who were ripping him off.

They sensed that, for Jack, the only challenge in the new operation was to maximize the profit margin and that, once attained, the only rewards would be economic and solely to Jack. The Unicorn Corporation never picked up on it until much after Jack had ripped them off for a pretty penny.

I posed as a bartender and, by the second night, I told Frank Angel I knew the score and could make a report. He berated me for being so naive and told me to say nothing for at least two, preferably three weeks before filing a report, as a two day assignment wasn't worth processing through his office. I normally would feel too conscientious to a client, particularly one such as a coffeehouse, to do such a thing, but Jack Sikking inspired such a total lack of feeling in his staff that I took Frank's advice and let it ride the whole three weeks.

In fact, I laid back and enjoyed it. I hired Paul George and Louie Martinez from the Westlake group to wash dishes, as they needed the coins, Paul inheriting my bartender's job as I moved on. When Jack had to serve food to qualify for a liquor license, I assisted him in the catering by establishing a minimum required menu of three dishes that our staff could handle: an overpriced snack plate of canned pate and breads, an overpriced cheese basket that still required no cooking and on which we made a fortune, and an outrageously exorbitant filet mignons, which I could cook if absolutely necessary and which was ordered only once by an undercover licensing inspector who complimented us on it.

Naturally, I cultivated the waitresses, taking them home at night together with a few bottles of Padre See California Champagne or Leibfraumilch, whichever we were overstocked with at the moment, and infrequently a couple of perfectly aged filet mignons which I convinced Jack had to be disposed of because of the questionable hint of blue lines in them.

Jack never thought to look in the trash cans at night, which is the means most dishonest employees in any business use to convey merchandise off the premises, as any boss would know if he'd trouble to hang around and see who retrieves the loot from the garbage after closing. Instead, the boss usually hires someone like Frank Angel who has someone like me watch the garbage can or work beside the shipping clerk whos mailing the stuff to himself at a dummy address or post office box.

The waitresses did not really have to confess anything to me in the intimacy of our after hours rendezvous; just watching them in the club playing games with the young friend Jack had put behind the register showed me how they could circumvent the various but futile cash systems Jack had used. The girls, and a few of the male staff, were more human than Jack and his friend, hence they were better psychologists, more resourceful, and, in a sense, more corruptible.

Before the first week ended, I had come up with specific dollar estimates which I ultimately learned were more accurate than both Jack's estimates, which he had withheld from me, or the girl's incomplete or exaggerated confessions. I was hard pressed at times to fulfill Frank Angel's waiting game since digging into the subject with the girls tended to make them more brazen in their efforts to steal.

On Odetta's closing night, she invited everyone over to her boyfriend Danny's house on Hoover. It was a modest old house, the kind they used to call 'shotgun houses' because the rooms were all in one line and with all the doors open you could shoot a shotgun through the length of the house without hitting anything. Danny had made a psychedelic pad out of it, murals and mosaics of vibrant colors and bits of colored bottle glass, mirror, and sequin vying with fabric and macrame to carry Daliesque designs from wall to ceiling to floor, from room to room with nothing to stop the flow of color except beaded curtains that alternated beads with spoons and forks and keys and miniature speakers that were hooked into the fabulous hi-fi system.

There was every kind of booze. There was a huge water pipe with six pipes terns to the circle of large multicolored velvet cushions around it, and a king's ransom of Columbian gold in a beautiful brass tea caddie that matched the hookah water pipe. There was an exquisite menorah with each of its nine candle drip cups holding a goodly supply of bennies, dexies, red dragons, and you name it. Would you believe, everybody got stoned.

Through my stupor, I saw Paul George making out with one of the waitresses, and just beyond them Jack Sikking was glaring daggers at his Nelly cash register friend who was idolizing Danny, who was the very embodiment of the saying 'black is beautiful.' The waitress was ecstasyzing over the horn of plenty Danny had provided and started comparing it to the wine and steaks we ripped off at the club. She was obviously headed toward discussing skimming the cash next, and

Jack was standing barely four feet from her reclining form. I signaled Paul with a finger across my throat to shut her up, but he was so stoned he just leered at me and returned his attention to her anatomy. The more she talked, the more Jack became tom between an interest in what she was saying and the interest his friend had in Danny. When Jack's attention definitely shifted to the waitress, I crawled over to where she lay entangled with Paul and clamped my mouth over hers in what I hoped looked like sex-crazed lust. Paul rose up on his elbows, frowned at me, and crawled off in indignation that I had intruded upon his new conquest. I looked out the comer of my eye to see Jack glaring suspiciously at me. His eyes were bloodshot and he was a little wobbly, so I hoped he'd forget his suspicions by the next day. I took my mouth off the girl's and said, "At least I didn't do what Danny's doing."

That did the trick. Jack whirled around to see his friend doing more of the doing than Danny, who was trying to make a polite retreat. Jack suddenly became more butch than I'd ever seen him. He steadied his thin impeccably dressed frame, ran both hands through his little bit of corn silk hair, and placed a bony but firm hand on his friend's collar, dragging him out of the house with stern pronouncements about overindulging in chemical vices.

As the girl put an arm around my neck and pulled me down on her so hard our teeth banged painfully, I ceased to worry about Jack's suspicions and began to worry about Paul thinking I had cut him out.

The next week at Theo Bikers opening, Theo brought a gorgeous young blonde in with him. She was over the age of consent, but definitely under the legal drinking age, and we were still being surveyed by the licensing people. She was enraptured with her "big Russian bear," and her big Russian bear kept letting her drink wine from stemmed glasses because she enjoyed smashing the empty glasses against the courtyard wall. Jack Sikking winced with each crash, fifty cents flashing in his eyeballs with each tinkle.

Theo Bikel was a part owner of Cosmo Alley and a Broadway, film, and recording star at the height of his career, and Jack was too intimidated to ask him to keep the girl out of sight, so he gave me that little job. After all, as Jack said, "What's a private investigator for if not to do someone's dirty work?" I wasn't keen on confronting the "big Russian bear," until I noticed the girl had decided to help out in the rush and was serving booze to tables, not only a threat to our licensing, but, if she started bringing back money from repeat or nonexistent receipts the thieving waitresses were using, their whole scam might be blown before I was able to turn in my report.

I took a double shot of the hot apple cider we kept in one side of the old fashioned twin coffee urns, and swaggered my five feet eleven inches over to Theo's six feet three inches as he tried to negotiate his balalaika and his abdomen through the dressing room door at the same time. As long as the girl was a witness, he roared protests to my reasoning that she should stay out of sight and liquorless, but, as soon as she was out of earshot, he turned into a pussycat and, with a shrug, said, "Don't tell her that you or Jack get busted because she's drinking. Tell her that I do, then she'll do anything you say," singing the last three words to the accompaniment of his balalaika as he strolled on stage. She drank her wine in the dressing room for the rest of the night, and the waitresses scored like mad with the heavy bread of Theo's opening.

Poor Jack had more trouble with his bosses like Theo Bikel and Herbie Cohen than he did with his thieving staff. Herbie, Mickey Cohen's nephew, was small but solid with dark curly hair. He made periodic visits to the club like any concerned owner should, and for the most part was quiet and unassuming. That is, until he opened his mouth, whereupon his ideas and the way they were expressed were invariably in conflict with the class atmosphere Jack was striving to attain.

During one of Herbie's visits, one of the waitresses came off the floor complaining that a customer was playing "grab-ass" with her, a frequent reaction to their provocative costumes. Herbie, who was shorter but heavier than Jack, walked over to him and blinked into Jack's ruffled shirt as he dispassionately said, "T'row de guy out."

Jack started to do his little hand dance and focused his disagreement on the girl with, "Don't be silly, darling, the man was just paying you a compliment. The poor thing probably wishes he had an ass as cute as yours."

Whereupon Herbie walked over to the client in question and said, "You! Out!"

The customer replied, "Fuck you!" as he stood up to his six foot height. Herbie quickly flashed a switchblade so big I wondered how a blade that looked like a broadsword could fit in that little tortoise-shell handle. With the switchblade point under the man's chin, Herbie led him like a dog on a leash out the front door without once drawing a drop of blood, finally booting him in the butt as the man half tripped into the gutter.

While the forever ex-customer ran down the street screaming obscenities and lawsuit threats, Jack stopped biting his fingernails long enough to say, "Herbie, I don't think you should've done that."

Herbie sidled up to the girl who had complained, saying, "Whad- daya mean? Nobody gooses my girls." Then he grabbed one of her buttocks so tightly she shut her eyes and held her breath until he said, "Right, baby?" As she turned a pained smile toward him, he released her buttock which began to show dark fingermarks through the pink leotard, and he left.

I was a little discomforted by those fingermark

bruises, as I had been spending a lot of time with that particular girl who was the current token olive-skin in the lineup, although she was actually Russian- Jewish. She stayed very healthy by studying modem dance, healthy enough to augment her living by posing nude for sculptors. I shared a lot with her, ate the bitter herbs with her family during the holidays, and would've accepted her invitation to move in with her, but for the fact that I couldn't take the endless parade of people she allowed to float through her house at all hours. Blind poets who didn't know if anyone was listening to their impromptu performances, spastic sculptors who wanted you to appraise their unidentifiable works of art, and folk singers, so many many folk singers, good and bad, but mostly bad. If only they had gone to school just long enough to learn how to tune their damn guitars.

What cooled our relationship was when she wanted me to throw Maxi out. Maxi was the a nutty young black jazz pianist who was immensely talented and who played the first three nights of the week at Cosmo Alley before the headliners who carried the four day weekend. His short, round, lightning fast presence was usually a total incongruity to the fantasies he was always acting out; practicing cowboy roping, playing fast draw with toy Flash Gordon rayguns, or doing the world's worst impressions of everyone from Bela Lugosi to Humphrey Bogart. Maxi had no home of his own. He was always mooching off of someone, and for a long time he had been living in her living room as a casual nightly drop-in. Of all the flaky deadbeats that crashed in her living room, he mooched most of all, but I was fondest of him because he was the only real talent.

At the keyboard he would parody Errol Garner or Oscar Peterson and you'd recognize the style, then you'd hear a counterpart that would take over and dominate the parody, and that was pure Maxi. He had the most disconcerting habit of humming the melody or counterpart loudly to himself while he played, but sometimes one to three beats behind or one to three halftones off key. I empathized with him because his hands were small and fingers short like mine, but I envied and admired him as a technician and talent far beyond my abilities as a pianist.

But he tore it with 'Miss Openhouse' when he ran up an unexpected fifty-dollar phone bill in business calls around the nation. She was fond of Maxi too, but she couldn't afford his eccentricities and wanted me to be the hatchet man. Fate saved me from that unpleasant task as Maxi's phone calls paid off and he was given a headline booking in San Francisco which led to a recording career under his legal name, Les McCann.

I soon turned in my report to Jack Sikking with recommendations as to how to retain most of the staff and three alternative cash systems that would preclude the skimming that had been going on. The first night under my new system, he grossed over a thousand dollars, more than double any previous gross he had recorded for a similar head count and indicative of far more skimming than he had dreamed.

Before the last of the staff had left that night, he puzzled them by approaching me with a blissful expression on his face, hugged and kissed me on both cheeks, and told me he'd give me a hundred dollar cash bonus. I suggested he give me Maxi's mid-week gig which had six weeks to run at the time Maxi left. Still hugging and smiling, he nodded affirmatively, "Sure."

"For scale," I added.

His smiling face kept wagging, "Sure," then slowed down together with his smile as he considered the difference between scale and the non-union wages he'd been paying mid-week performers. When the smile and the hug wound down to his usual supercool self, he added, "Of course, you realize this precludes the hundred-dollar bonus."

I hugged him, put my smiling face close to his and said, "Of course."

He yanked himself away from me and said, straightening his expensive slim-Jim tie, "Don't forget to sweep up before you close," and minced away.

All this time I had been trying to sell Lenny on the idea of playing Cosmo Alley as it was really becoming a classy nightclub rather than the beatnik haunt he had known it to be when Benny Shapiro opened it. When it came to beatniks, Lenny liked the grass and the girls, but he preferred the clothes and cologne of the show-biz crowd for his own image. He didn't really know the stature of Josh White and Odetta, but when Theo Bikel bought in and started appearing there, that equated with Broadway and movies to him, and he began to prod me to promote the booking.

After my assignment with Frank Angel was over, yet still affiliated with Cosmo Alley as a performer, be it ever so humbly the mid-week pianist, I was free to sell Lenny to Jack, who only knew Lenny from what he'd read of the Slate Brothers fiasco in *Variety.* I showed him the album on the Fantasy label, *The Sick Humor of Lenny Bruce,* with my cover, and played him select portions, carefully editing out any references to gays which, while very fair and supportive in reality, I didn't know how Jack would take. Jack bought it, but dickered over money. I got Lenny less than Theo got, but considerably more than he got for the Slate Brothers gig.

I begged Lenny not to repeat the Slate Brothers mistake, not for my sake, because I didn't value the few weeks I had left as a pianist that much, but for his career's sake. I got him to promise that if he got nervous or the audience got nasty, he'd just take a dive, bow out without attacking the audience, and see how he felt about the next show or the next night.

He had no problems. I think he had gained a lot of confidence just from the release of the album as well as the little trickle of positive response we had gotten from it at that point. He didn't know it, but I had a better claque going for him then I could manipulate at the Slate Brothers club. I carefully peppered the audience with members of the staff, Paul George swapping his dishwasher's apron for a coat and tie to join the rest, and coached them as to the punch lines that needed accents of applause or laughter. Whether it helped or was totally unnecessary is hard to say, because Lenny was so much better than most of his previous performances that I think he was as happily surprised as I was at the success of that booking.

The Cosmo Alley gig did not bring national recognition, but it helped legitimize Lenny's nightclub track record after the stigma of the Slate Brothers incident. Most important, it helped me convince Lenny that coffeehouses constituted an 'underground' platform particularly suited to his brand of social satire, and his acceptance of this helped pave the way to subsequent bookings that brought him national attention.

Chapter 7
FRIENDS AND LOVERS

Friends and lovers are what determine the true course and perhaps the ultimate worth of our life, as most spiritual philosophies try to tell us in many different ways. It is our one to one relationships that determine the quality, or lack of it, in our life's experience. So it behooves us to select and nurture them with care.

There's an old Hollywood saying, "Be good to everyone on the way up, because you never know who you'll meet on the way down." Very practical if not compassionate, but most people who get to the top not only feel the rule no longer applies to them, they often feel downright vindictive to those they feel slighted them on the way up. Frankie used to say to Lenny, particularly after we started filming and the diversity of my talents began to appear, "Wouldn't it be funny if the kid made it before we did?" Well, the 'kid' didn't make it before them and may never 'make it' as far as Oscars and big bucks, but I'm not dead yet, either.

Frankie was always ready to take a back seat. He was not a fighter, despite the fact that his younger brother had been a boxer and his parents feisty. They were a short cutesy couple from Calabria in the old country, the father pretending to speak no English when I'd visit for dinner. The old man would make disparaging remarks about 'show people' in Italian peppered with obscene vocabulary. Frankie once dropped his fork halfway to his mouth when, after I had just complimented the food, his father said in Italian, "He's so damn polite he'd probably compliment you if you fed him raw mountain oysters," only he used more earthy terminology.

As I screwed up my face with restrained laughter, Frankie cleaned his spattered tie and implored his father, "Dad, the kid knows a little Italian just like you know a little English, ya'know." Whereupon his mother added in Italian, completely unruffled by the exchange and without losing a stroke with her fork, "Your father's right, ya'know, he probably would compliment you no matter what kind of slop you served him. He's a good boy."

I said, "Grazie."

Mamma said, "You're welcome," between continuous fork fulls, and the old man dropped his fork and glared at Frankie who shook his head cockily and gloated.

I don't know where or when Frankie had become resigned to conceding the limelight. Maybe his parents had always disapproved of his profession and he wanted to prove them right, but I saw it when I first met Frankie in New Orleans and he had just started taking a back seat to Shecky's career. Shecky had taken off on tour and left Frankie to nurse their investment in The Wit's End club.

Frankie continued in this direction as his title of 'partner' to Shecky spiraled downward to 'associate' and then 'writer.' When we decorated those Beverly Hills offices for Shecky, it was to house Shecky's corporation which Frankie managed and called Who's He. When we all saw Lord Buckley doing pioneer comedy albums and Lenny and I began to package Lenny's work, Frankie produced Shecky's first comedy album titled *Shecky In The Lounge* compiled from tapes of Shecky's early Las Vegas performances and a cover showing Shecky dressing in the lady's lounge where his wife Gerry and other women ignored his presence while they put on makeup.

I think Frankie started grooming Lenny because he was starting to feel insecure with Shecky. Shecky was unproven and unstable at the time, but Frankie had a streak of loyalty that would have lasted through all the hell

Shecky went through and more. I think Frankie felt he was being eased out of Shecky's career, possibly by Gerry, possibly through other factors.

When I left the Nick Lucas project with Frankie to start working almost exclusively with Lenny, I think Frankie thought he might again be displaced, this time from Lenny's career. When we started filming *The Leather Jacket* three months later and Frankie and I started talking again, I quickly reassured him that was not the case. I distinctly remember a conversation we had one night after leaving Canter's, one of the many rap sessions we had sitting in Frankie's little black Rambler Metropolitan convertible (a poor man's sports car) with the top down on a warm California night. I was reassuring Frankie he was still number one with Lenny, and Frankie was bemoaning the circuitous course of his own career.

He always used to blame it on his legs. He'd say, "The legs are the first to go, ya'know, for a standup comic. It's like a boxer, you ain't got legs and you can't dance no more, can't duck the punches. My legs hurt. I stand up there on stage in that toilet, ushering cooze on and offstage night after night, nobody's listening when I do something that's never been done before. Who knows if it's great or not if nobody listens? The other night I couldn't take it no more, I nearly swallowed the mike shouting at them. I said, 'Shut up, you schmucks, there's a comedy routine going on up here, a hundred and sixty pounds of talent with twenty years experience in the business of trying to cast a few pearls before you swine.'" He sighed heavily and looked up at the stars. "Ya'know, kid, for the first time in a long time they shut up and listened to me, and all I could think of was that my legs hurt." He looked down and shook his head. "No, kid, I gotta give my legs a rest, gotta hitch my wagon to somebody else's star; Shecky's, Lenny's, somebody's."

I don't recall ever seeing Frankie cry, although I

think he wanted to at that moment. I know I did. Instead I played 'hail fellow well met' and chided him, "Hey, man, where's the guy who wrote me that Hollywood was our oyster, the guy who was gonna write and direct movies with me, the guy that argued with me about who'd walk up to accept the Oscars?"

Frankie pulled his little Rhett Butler string bow tie loose. "I don't know. That guy got lost somewhere back along the way; Hollywood, Juarez, the French Quarter. Somewhere back there his legs started to give out and he can't even stand up on a toilet burlesque house stage, much less the Academy podium."

Frankie and I both had a slight aversion to physical contact with other males, but he didn't flinch when I put my arm around him and said, "No, he's not lost. He's right here with me and we're making our first movie just like we said we'd do several years ago."

He looked out from under those bushy eyebrows at me as he pulled the string tie out of his collar and said, "It ain't our movie, it's Lenny's."

I have had few close friends in my life, but certainly, though there are years at a time that I don't see him, Frankie is one of the truest and closest, having shared some of my highest dreams and hopes and some of my lowest depths of disappointment. I am equally sure Frankie was Lenny's finest friend, perhaps not as intimately as Honey or Joe Maini, but Frankie's recognition, faith, and nurturing of Lenny's talent was proof of a quality of friendship Lenny desperately needed, that he got from no other source, and without which Lenny Bruce would not be known to the world today.

On the other end of Lenny's spectrum of male friends was Joe Maini, perhaps his most intimate male friend and, ironically, the most destructive element in Lenny's life and career. Lenny was enamored of jazz musicians and Joe was a highly lauded saxophonist, an intimate of Charlie Parker and other jazz greats. Lenny met Joe shortly before meeting Frankie and me, at which point Joe had given up any serious musical career to become a pimp and pusher to support his long established drug habit. Lenny had experimented with lesser drugs prior to meeting Joe, and perhaps Lenny was destined to be a drug abuser, but it was Joe who gets credit for teaching him to mainline heroin.

Joe had a beautiful and exotic girlfriend, Sandra, whom he introduced to drugs while still in her teens, and he peddled her body to support their mutual habit. He was the center of a drug circle, mostly jazz musicians, and his relationship with Sandra probably began as a sincere love relationship, but degenerated as they both became physically and mentally ill from drug addiction. He was not a typical pimp, but their circumstances were fairly typical of most hookers and their pimps. They were at one time or another victimized by customers, pushers, organized crime, and the police. Like many girls I've known in the business, Sandra was physically abused, robbed, extorted, and paid her dues to vice officers singly and in groups.

I once heard Joe tell the story about the time he and Sandra went to Tijuana to score some dope, didn't get the dope, but got cheated out of their money instead. Without funds to return to Los Angeles, Sandra picked up a trick on the street who turned out to be a Mexican vice officer. She learned that paying dues to vice officers in Mexico was worse than in the States.

At the time, Joe was shook up about the incident, but I knew him long enough to see him add it to an endless litany of such stories which he and Lenny came to regard as funny or adventurous, like two teenage boys gleefully recounting their various adventures in the rites of manhood.

Joe was very cagey with me. He knew I was

strictly straight on dope, but he also knew Lenny and I had a strong professional association which Lenny valued, so Joe was cordial with me. When I was around he always acknowledged me, laughed at my jokes even if they were often less than hip, and, if it were a more private gathering of a more swinging group, he'd introduce girls to me.

I was always wary around girls Joe introduced to me. I assumed they were more than likely hookers, and they mostly were. Pretty and pathetic, it seemed they all had come from nowhere after one or two teenage pregnancies, usually out of wedlock, the offspring now adopted or with their parents or grandparents, come to tinsel town to be a movie star or at the very least a model, and been robbed, raped, or ripped off to one degree or another before great father-pimp-protec- tor Joe or whoever had taught them the ropes, which always included hooking and usually included drowning their sorrows in junk. Now they could tell fascinating stories about the celebrities they had balled, which ones wore girdles to keep their manly tummies flat, which ones had false hair and teeth, which ones needed coke to get it up, and which ones needed to abuse or humiliate them. They never bothered to mention the ninety-nine less glamorous tricks they turned for every one that was a 'worthy' encounter. They wore long sleeves or cute tattoos to hide the needle tracks on their arms. They turned the lights off if there were welts on their bodies from a recent customer. But nothing could hide the vacant look in a girl's eyes after her pimp has told her that she's no longer grade 'A' goods, that she looks ten years older than her years, that she's now just another piece of meat that has to make up in quantity what she's lost in quality. She shows you a crumpled picture of herself as a cheerleader, as a local bathing beauty queen, as a 4-H winner with her prize lamb. She yearns for you to tell her she is still that beautiful, that wholesome, that full of promise, but she can't even remember whether she was instructed to fuck you for free as a favor to her pimp or bring him the money.

At one point I was about to lose the studio, having worked primarily on *The Leather Jacket* without any returns and having failed to collect delinquent accounts like the little dance record company next door. Lenny was frantically trying to help me retain the studio without my having to take a time-consuming job which would cut into our projects. Joe Maini suggested I become a pimp and Lenny thought that would be a perfect solution. After all, I was always playing 'Dutch Uncle' to dancers and actresses and performers whether they were straight or full time or part time hookers. Why shouldn't I receive some reward, other than sex, for such counseling, which merely required me to counsel them to be hookers?

When I hesitated, Joe decided to send me a ready made hooker so I wouldn't have to corrupt some innocent young thing. I can't even remember the girl's name, only that she was, like Dolores in El Paso, a French Canadian. Beyond her height and square jaw, however, she was totally unlike Dolores in looks and personality. This woman had to be ten years older than me, one of the rejects from Joe's or someone's stable. She was only passably attractive. She said she had just come to town from Canada, but conversation revealed she had made the rounds of most of Hollywood's celebrity market which, in her case, meant most of the older, more jaded or difficult customers. She agreed to work any market I developed for her, which I thought would have to be totally apart from the entertainment industry to preserve my integrity there. More of my theorizing on the subject made it plain to her that I was a rank amateur at being a pimp and, in fact, was trying to place too many obstacles in the way because I didn't really want to go through with it. She saw quite plainly I was not going to take command of her life nor put her to work, so she ended up borrowing half of my last twenty dollars on the pretext of some immediate need she had, probably a fix, and I never saw her again.

Lenny and I had almost entirely different attitudes towards women.

He liked his women to not be 'ladies.' He wanted them to appear, as he would put it, 'hot,' or, as I would put it, wanton and licentious. He liked the makeup and attire one normally associates with a flamboyant streetwalker, a taste I suspect he acquired seeing such streetwalkers during his childhood in New York or the similar type of stage makeup and costuming on female performers early in his show-biz career. While driving down the street, he would nearly cause accidents screaming or grasping my arm for attention to be focused on some garishly made up and costumed girl on the sidewalk, making me circle the block two or more times to observe her, though he rarely had the courage to accost her under those circumstances without the showbiz trappings around him to impress her.

Lenny had more than average hostility to women, born probably more from his conflicts with his wife than with his mother, and relating to women as prostitutes gave him an advantage he felt he needed. He always reserved the option to dismiss a woman as if she were a paid employee whenever the slightest conflict arose. The only concession he made was to lie outrageously to them until they were seduced; thereafter, concessions were granted only in proportion to their celebrity status and its value to his ego.

Like Lenny, I was raised in a predominantly female household, but the environment was more provincial and conservative. For a variety of reasons, I think I had more opportunity to maintain a perspective on women who, despite any distinctions imposed by society or tradition, were each an individual human to be accorded the same civil rights and individuality I expected for myself.

Lenny had another friend who I suspect was an

innately good and constructive element in his life from before the time I met him. Sandra Barton had a casual relationship with Lenny in the East before she came out to Hollywood in the late fifties with her husband, Chris, and small daughter, Noel. Sally brought her to me as a performer in need of pictures and as a dear friend. I loved her humor, her blatant honesty, and what Honey called her 'pixie good looks.' Sandy hung with me until Chris and Noel arrived and, at one point, we all lived together in a little rear cottage on Lillian Street behind what was then Desilu Studios. In our mutual survival society, I clued them into the thrift shops from which we furnished our homes and filled our wardrobes, the USC School of Dentistry where we got our free dental work done, and the Hollywood Barber School where we got free haircuts.

Chris was a beautiful man in looks and nature, but haunted by a Medusa of misadventures in life from the blow to his vanity of middle age balding, to the nightmares from which he woke screaming about the several times his ships had been torpedoed while in the merchant marine during W orld War II. I tried helping him keep house while Sandy was performing on the road as 'Mistress of Comedy and Song.' I tried helping him procure and fulfill housepainting contracts to bring in money. And I tried interesting him in writing, but Chris's writing was too morbid and obtuse for me to collaborate on and the complexity of his other problems was more than I, and I suspect Sandy, could hope to help him with.

But it was through Sandy that I began for the first time to get a handle on Lenny's past and his relationship with Honey. I found Sandy a fair and open person without the presumption to judge anyone. While Lenny and Sally were not necessarily down on Honey, they could not be considered objective or even very communicative on the subject.

Honey was the mystery lady with invisible strings

on Lenny that tugged him in unexpected directions when I'd least expect, and I couldn't figure out why until I began to get the picture from Sandy. Honey's presence was strongly felt, even though she had just begun a two year drug sentence at San Pedro when I started working with Lenny.

That presence was most noticeable in all things related to another of Lenny's ladies, the only one I gave my heart completely to or let influence my work with him. That was Kitty, his daughter, who was about three then; exquisite, lovable, and precocious. She looked like the little girl on the old Campbell soup ads with a Dutch boy haircut and a cherub's face. In my teens I had grown sick of taking baby pictures for a living, but I photographed Kitty so enthusiastically you'd think she was my daughter, which subconsciously I think was the way I felt about her.

Lenny had an older woman as his housekeeper. Lucille was a kindly, super straight woman who was practically deaf and had no idea of her employer's notoriety or the impertinent things he said to her when her hearing aid was turned down, which always embarrassed Frankie and me. Frankie's brows would raise quizzically as he'd say, "Lenny, you shouldn't say things like that to the poor old lady."

Lenny would make the snuffling sound that preceded a short, high pitched cackle and say, "Yeah, but ain't it funny thinking of her doing that to me?"

Frankie's rejoinder was, "What would really be funny was if she heard you and actually did it."

I bitterly added, "Or she heard you and dumped that bowl of soup on your head." Frankie and Lenny looked at each other the way they did when something unexpected popped out of me.

There were two types of situations where I felt the desire, the need, and to some degree the right to challenge Lenny; when we were collaborating on a project, and when

I was in the home environment he provided for Kitty. The housekeeper provided a sane, stable, and loving environment for the child, but beyond that, I sometimes challenged Lenny on Kitty's behalf, about many of the friends and associates who entered his home, and his interaction with them. I myself have some pretty liberal attitudes about child rearing, but included in there is the belief that a child is capable of perceiving adult behavior and that a parent is obliged to invest the time, energy, and sacrifices necessary to monitor and manage at least the child's home environment. Lenny and Honey were not unlike so many parents who did not anticipate, accept, or fulfill the responsibilities of having a child, but once separated, wanted to control the child in part to manipulate and hurt the spouse.

Because he knew I loved to be around Kitty, Lenny conned me into regularly driving the housekeeper and Kitty down to San Pedro to visit Honey. The more I knew about Honey and Lenny's relationship, the more I realized Lenny was approaching a crisis about what to do when Honey got out, and it was coming right at the time his career started its greatest upswing.

Shortly before Honey was to be released, Lenny and I had one of our periodic serious discussions about long term projections for his career. He asked me what I thought about the Honey situation and I told him how I saw it. I said, "Legally and publicity wise, you risk an immense liability to your person and certainly your career if you remain married to Honey. If you divorce her, but still love her and want to be with her, explain your reasons to her fully before you initiate anything. If you want to be with her, maintain a separate legal residence for yourself, even if you spend 100% of your time at Honey's residence, and your housekeeper can maintain your legal residence as Kitty's home because Honey should have one or two years to get her act together before she assumes any more responsibility than visitation rights to Kitty, for Honey's sake as well as Kitty's. But let Kitty know her mother, let there be no doubt as to her mother's love for her nor denial to Honey of her daughter's expression of love for her."

I remember it well because I had said these things over and over to myself driving back and forth to San Pedro with Kitty and seeing Lenny vacillate back and forth between being so bitter towards Honey he wanted to cut her off entirely, and alternately yearning so for her that he wanted to set up house with her and Kitty and Joe Maini and all the entourage that kept floating through the La Brea apartment to broaden Kitty's education a bit prematurely.

I remember it well because I remember my mother's wisdom when, as a divorcee with three children during the Great Depression, she didn't let her reasons to be bitter prejudice her children; she let us know our father and understand the benefits that came from both parents and whatever material or personal advantages either of them could voluntarily offer. I remember it well because it was the very issue over which, less than a month later, Lenny would do the only overtly unkind thing he ever did to me.

Two days before Honey was to get out of prison, which was three days before he needed to leave for an important booking at the Hungry I in San Francisco, Lenny left town and sent me a note via Sally instructing me to take Kitty down to Honey in San Pedro and then set the two of them up permanently in his La Brea apartment. I told Sandy Barton I couldn't do it because, for one, I didn't think that setup was good for anyone concerned, as Lenny well knew (and I suspect left me the chore as a personal sting), and two, I rather think he anticipated I'd get involved with Honey her first night out and guilt would soften the edge of the sword I was honing for him.

Sandy and Chris got a good looking drummer from the club Sandy was working in, picked up Honey at San

Pedro the next day, and the four of them partied all night. I did not want to reject Honey, and the following day I took her to my bank to cash some large bonds she had, took her shopping for a red Thunderbird convertible which she just had to have, and bought a lot of gift-wrapped kiddie presents because it was Christmas eve.

At one point in our shopping, I had to leave my car to be serviced and we decided to catch a bus to our next destination. Buses in Los Angeles are like taxis in New York on a rainy day, nonexistent. A very large, good looking black guy approached us with some story about chauffeuring us in exchange for gas in his car so he could take his children for a ride on Christmas day. We took him for the fuzz, but thought, what the hell, let the vice squad chauffeur us if they want to because we're cool. The guy went for his car and pulled up in a triple tone lavender Lincoln Continental. His name was Mike and the rest of the day convinced us he wasn't a cop (in fact, in the years after I learned he was anything but).

By the end of the day we had gotten everything except a Christmas tree. Mike and I scoured the tree lots, but at that late hour they were all closed. On our way back to the apartment we spied a beautifully decorated Christmas tree ornamenting the landscaped front of a famous Wilshire Boulevard department store. We parked and waited for the security guard to show. As soon as the guard made his round and left, we stole the tree which almost completely hid the lavender Lincoln once we got it tied on top. We got it up the stairwell to the apartment, but had to keep lopping sections off the bottom to get it inside. Our efforts were rewarded with Kitty's ecstatic approval.

As I admired the spellbinding beauty of Honey and Kitty that Christmas eve, I pondered how unpredictable and vulnerable our lives were, each buffeted up and down by the virtues and liabilities of our circumstances and personal and professional relationships. What direction

119

would Lenny's life have taken had he not met Honey and Joe Maini or Frankie and me? Where would my talents have applied themselves had I not met Frankie and Lenny? And what did the future hold for this exquisite child whose beauty outshone the angel atop the tree and who Lenny used as a pawn in his power struggles with Honey and with me?

Chapter 8
POWER CORRUPTS

As I sit writing these pages decades later, I am obliged to consider that many readers did not experience the sixties and may find it difficult to understand how the satirical comedy of Lenny Bruce could have such social impact or, for that matter, why a reasonably intelligent soul such as myself would persevere in the face of Lenny's obvious failings in personal and professional relations.

Many would consider Lenny's material tame compared to a Richard Pryor or a George Carlin, taking for granted the freedom of expression that comedians and most performers in all media enjoy today. Many of today's readers were children or infants or not even born, and therefore could not be aware of, much less run afoul of, the repression and conformity of that time.

Just as our bodies carry forth the evolutionary remnants of a vestigial tail at the base of the spine and a reptilian brain beneath our larger brain, so America dragged forth into the beginning of the sixties unconstitutional laws discriminating against twenty million black Americans, unconstitutional laws repressing one hundred million female Americans, and the tendency of political, social, and religious leaders to invoke those laws to maintain the general and their particular status quo, for better or for worse.

This was a time when laws prohibited a black child from drinking at a white drinking fountain in Georgia and prohibited a black man from walking the streets of Pasadena, California, after ten in the evening. This was a time when a woman was guilty of provoking rape if her breasts and buttocks were allowed to jiggle free of a superstructured bra and girdle. This was a time when one of the largest television viewing audiences watched a Catholic priest who espoused conservative policies, endorsed right-wing politicians, and turned a blind eye to the growing indignation of the public who resented the excesses of its leaders.

It was a time of two-valued thinking: black or white, good or evil, for or against. If you were not for God (preferably the Christian God), then you must be an ally of Satan; if you opposed your political leaders, then you must be a proponent of Communism and therefore a traitor; if you practiced miscegenation (the legal term then used in some states for interracial sex), then you went against the founding fathers, who obviously did not intend for their democratic experiment to extend to their black slaves and neighboring American Indians.

These inequities were not unique to the fifties or sixties. Presidents, potentates, and popes had invoked such controls upon society for millennia in the misguided and selfish belief that civilization should evolve in their own national, racial, or religious image. What was astounding was that these contradictions of the great American experiment in democracy had prevailed through a half-century of growing mass media.

For it is timing that is the distinction of a prophet; not piety or perfection. It takes but a seed of honesty planted in the spring of awareness to grow into a tree of knowledge. A single pearl of wisdom might jostle amidst millions to find the perfect niche for its perfect symmetry. The smallest spark of genius may illuminate the world only if it chances to ignite a powerful source of energy. Those particles of honesty, wisdom, and genius in Lenny have been possessed in larger or smaller degrees by countless people, but Lenny happened to possess them in the late spring of his life, in the niche of show business's mass media, and in the ignitable atmosphere of social revolution which was the sixties.

The cry for freedom that ultimately issued from Lenny had long bubbled within the breasts of bohemians and beatniks, me and my peers, and millions who did not want to give up their lives or the quality of their lives to ensure their leader's names in history books for wars won or deities appeased. While others voiced that cry in loftier impassioned speeches on the steps of churches and capitals, Lenny voiced that same cry through the entertainment media concerning real issues and real people. But Lenny was not running for office. He was just an innocent who saw reality in a very talented way, and found it funny that 'the emperor wore no clothes.'

That was Lenny's most unique talent, the courage and/or naivete to joust with the dragons plaguing society. Whether he was St. George or Don Quixote is debatable, but he fought the good fight all of us wanted to, but few dared. That is why the likes of Frankie and I stood by him despite his obvious faults. His injustices against us were insignificant compared to the social injustices he attacked early in his career and the personal injustices ultimately heaped upon him.

I do not claim to have been fully conscious of such insight when I was twenty-three and first met Lenny. Frankie regarded him primarily as an exceptional performing talent, one that he could appreciate and aid with his own perception, experience, and talents far better than his show business peers who simply regarded Lenny as a dirty joke. I didn't even have Frankie's perception of Lenny's talent. I only knew that, while I enjoyed storytelling with Frankie, writing with Lenny was 'meaningful' storytelling. At twenty-three I was consciously searching for answers as to why society was a spider web of hypocrisies. Writing with Lenny, I found I could take a stick to the spider web and taunt the spider.

Neither Frankie nor Lenny nor I realized how

dangerous it was to play with spider webs. Lenny certainly did not intend to risk his career and his life embarking on social crusades. And I certainly did not intend to commit ten years of my time and talents to a man who not only fought corruption, but was himself so very vulnerable and corruptible.

We are all potentially corruptible, and I heard one really sweet guy confess to a vulnerable moment in which he succumbed to corruption. Joe E. Ross visited Frankie Ray at the Near And Far one evening and spent the whole night rapping with the gang at Canter's. On the way back to his car with Frankie and me he did a little soul searching.

He knew he was born with a funny face and voice and enough talent to earn the success he'd had as a nightclub comic through the years, but he knew his career had long since reached a plateau when his friend, Phil Silvers, did him the favor of including him in *The Sgt. Bilko Show.* He also knew it was a fluke that his difficulty in learning his part, resulting in his characteristic "ooooh ooooh," was what made him stand out as the army cook in the series and eventually got him his show, *Car 54 Where Are You?*

When the conversation between us got around to girls, Joe told us of an incident where the assistant director noticed that Joe had been partying with one of the girls on the show in his dressing room trailer while doing the series. The fellow was a crass type and asked Joe if he'd "make" the girl give him a "quickie." Joe was startled to think that anyone would have the power to do that, and, largely out of curiosity, he "told" the girl to "do" the assistant director. To Joe's amazement, she did. Joe immediately felt remorse and promptly made the assistant director give the girl three extra days work.

I myself am no stranger to vulnerability, temptation, and remorse.

In this book alone, I have confessed how tempted and close I came at times to being a purse snatcher and a pimp. I will further admit that in the course of my life I have grappled with the temptation to be a thief, a prostitute, and an accomplice in fraud, and I have not always won the battle. I can only say for myself that, in proportion to the vast amount of temptation I have been exposed to, I have succeeded in resisting such temptations more than 95% of the time.

The acid tests I put such temptations to are, in increasing order of importance: 1. How hard have I tried to rationalize this act? 2. How profoundly and permanently will it affect my external relations with my peers and society in general? 3. How profoundly and permanently will it affect my evaluation of myself, for ultimately I am the final judge of the quality of my life and my person?

If in Korea I stole excess rations from the Air Force to help my Korean girlfriend avoid starving, I could live with that. If in Jamaica I had lunch on the yacht of a gay executive from America's leading advertising agency in order to pitch the Pancho Villa and Johnny Aladdin series, even though I didn't play and the agency didn't pay, I could live with that. If at Melrose and Vine I was party to Lenny's deluding a bigoted clergyman, I could live with that.

In those cases, I was the little guy, the Air Force and ad executive and clergyman were the people in power. I may or may not have been guilty of choosing the wrong response, but I was not guilty of having been corrupted by power. There is always the possibility that had I obtained power in similar situations, I too might have been corrupted, but I'm inclined to think that my experiences as the little guy would help me avoid that mistake.

Perhaps Lenny's being an only child kept him from ever thinking of himself as 'the little guy." Maybe that was part of his naivete which led him to joust with dragons, oblivious to the consequences. Perhaps, too, it contributed to his being selfish at times, and vulnerable to being corrupted by his success.

Lenny had played Ann's 440 Club in San Francisco, another coffeehouse type nightclub, and had begun to gain national attention because of the public relations efforts of that club's management and the resulting good reviews in San Francisco. In due time, Steve Allen 'discovered' him, loved his social satire, and put him on his television program, *The Steve Allen Show*. Likewise, Hugh Hefner identified overtly with Lenny's reference to sexual openness and honesty, and covertly with Lenny's drug culture, putting him on *The Playboy Penthouse* television show and running a *Playboy* magazine article on him entitled *Rebel With A Caustic Cause*, showing Lenny from the *Religions Incorporated* routine as the snake-wielding, dirt-floor preacher, "Here, boy, have a snake."

When Lenny returned to Los Angeles in 1959 to play the Crescendo on Sunset, the 'class' club at that time, he started building a palatial house in the Hollywood Hills. He and I went over the architect's drawings making modifications for some of the touches Lenny wanted incorporated in the house, which began to show me some details about Lenny's character that I had previously only guessed at.

We bugged the entire house with permanently installed mikes and line amps built into the walls, using wireless bugs in the pool and patio areas. We converted one tiny downstairs room into a master control room equipped with banks of recorders that could be used to make transfers or to record from any area of the house simultaneously and independently. Despite the fact that he still owed me back pay and percentages from the past two years, we spent a fortune equipping him with every known concealed recording equipment, from pocket sized recorders with wristwatch microphones to my personally designed custom made attache case with concealed external mike and controls for the recorder contained within. If it sang, spoke, spit, or slurped, we could bug it.

For a house that size, there was a noticeable lack of kitchen facilities, the two small kitchens upstairs and downstairs were never fully equipped and more often used as offices or storage. Lenny lived on deli food, didn't know how to cook himself, and didn't want anyone around him devoting that much attention to preparing food.

The bedrooms, of which there were many including the huge upstairs living room which was decorated as a bedroom, were mirrored and built for entertaining. They were never furnished with much more than mattresses and huge puff pillows. While at home, Lenny lived in bedrooms and bathrooms. He liked to sprawl in the center of the bed wearing pajamas or a robe and hold court with everyone sitting on pillows or on the floor encircling him. The bed and room were always littered with takeout food bags, soiled clothing, and, in later years, photocopied pages of court transcript.

The bathrooms brought up one of the unspoken barriers between us. In each there were three fixtures piped in purple velvet beside the toilet. One was a toilet paper fixture with a roll of toilet paper in it. The second was a toilet paper fixture with a roll of tear-off envelopes containing disposable hypodermic syringes. The third, at the bottom of the row, was a square hole in the wall with a freefall path down to the concrete building foundation so used syringes could not be easily recovered as evidence.

I had only two conversations with Lenny about drugs. The first was during the initial year I worked with him and we finished a writing session one night with yet another invitation from him to go over to Joe Maini's and meet some more "spaced-out broads." I previouswly had junkie friends in the French Quarter, the Orient, and Mexico, and had seen them transgress every moral standard and ethic of friendship and humanity in their hour of need. I read the few books available then on the subject to try to help them withdraw, only to see them convulse and turn gray and green and blue, and sometimes die, but never seem able to kick the addiction. I was afraid of drugs and of Joe Mainis environment, and I told Lenny so that night, adding, by reason of a fair amount of experience, that I felt "Anyone over twenty who'd been on hard stuff more than two years was an incurable member of the walking dead."

Despite my experience, and despite his intimacy with Joe who was such an avowed junkie, I was too joyously involved with the work Lenny and I were doing together to consider he might be using drugs, until that night, however, when he noticeably stiffened at my remark and coolly promised never to embroil me in Joe Maini's business again.

We never mentioned drugs again, even when I altered the house plans for the little bathroom fixtures, until more than eight years later, a year before he died. I suppose it was naive of me, after all that had happened by then, to ask him why he never drove anymore and had John Judnich chauffeur him everywhere. He had just opened the gate for me as I returned with some food from Canter's because John wasn't there at the moment to fetch it for him. We sat on the patio, I in my eternal black clothes and he in his eternal terrycloth bathrobe, and the sun set over his spectacular view of the city while we ate. Without flinching or a hint of malice in his voice he said, "I don't drive anymore because I'm a dope fiend, and a dope fiend is a menace on the road and a target for police harassment." He took a big bite of food and handed the bag to me with a smile on his face. He hadn't accented the words "dope fiend," but I knew he had used them because he half suspected that's the context I thought of drug users in, including him.

I smiled as I took the bag and replied, "If you say so, Lenny," while I dug into the goodies.

But back when the house was first being built and he was living in a rented house on Gower, I began to see a parallel between the indiscretions he allowed to creep into Kitty's home environment and the indiscretions he was committing in his artistic and business relationship with Frankie and me. Lenny had some rather selfish priorities that outranked his commitment to Kitty, so it wasn't that surprising that they outranked his commitments to Frankie and me, and they came damn close to outranking any commitment to his whole career.

There were countless little things that at first Frankie and I attributed to the 'Will-Success-Spoil-Rock-Hunter' syndrome. He began to see less of us socially. He no longer introduced us to celebrities or business contacts as his "associates" or "collaborators." He began to opt for the company of hangers-on who were willing to wear a visored cap and pretend to be his chauffeur or accept his addressing them as domestics and go-fers.

But well into the first year of his big success, the third year of our association, I discovered he had given the original footage of *The Leather Jacket* to a rank amateur to edit "creatively" at his own discretion, practically destroying the entire project. I discovered he had re-typed the cover pages of the three scripts we had co-authored to change my credit to "camera setups by" and "additional dialogue by" before registering them. He was becoming increasingly secretive about his finances, lying to us about his true income, and there was some indication he had collected for my album cover photographs from the record company without paying me. And to top it all, while our collaborative projects were floundering for want of even shoestring capital, I discovered he was spending huge sums on personal luxuries like drugs and ego-tripping with parties for his entourage.

For several months I had been holding on by a thread to try to keep Lenny's basket of eggs intact, while Frankie and I both had passed up offers to work on independent films in Arizona, Mexico, Texas, and New Orleans. Frankie had also jeopardized his professional association with Shecky Greene in focusing on Lenny's career. The two of us were not only seeing little or no bread from it all, we were seeing less and less cooperation from Lenny who was partying more and more. I went gunning for Lenny and he started ducking me.

Lenny stayed on the road for months and, by the time he returned, Honey had moved to a cottage in Hollywood she shared with a butch looking Chinese girl. The police were in the habit of showing up at the door with search warrants, and Kitty, who was barely old enough to open the door for them, was getting used to a rather exciting life at a very early age.

Frankie knew I wanted to confront Lenny and told me I'd be able to catch both him and Lenny over at Honey's cottage that day on the occasion of her latest hassle with the police. I arrived to see Kitty wandering around puzzled by and unnoticed in the confusion. Lenny hadn't expected me and felt uptight about a lot of different things.

I told him I wanted physical possession of *The Leather Jacket* project for the purpose of trying to salvage and complete it, or I wanted him to buy back my contracts and unpaid accounts with him for fifty cents on the dollar. He said he was "tap city, stony broke," but I had verified that day his house was still in construction and he was booked for months prior and after that date at no less than $7500 a week. Neither would he give me *The Leather Jacket* footage. He kept saying, "I'll finish the film just as soon as I get a few more bucks. You're still in for everything I promised." He began to blink and blow through his nose, looking down at the ground and then up with a pained smile on his face.

Through clenched teeth I said, "I notice I'm in now as 'camera setups by' and 'additional dialogue by.'"

He looked up at the sky and laughed nervously, "Heh heh heh, that's only for marquee value when I go looking for more investors. They want a known name on it to sell it and they gotta believe I have complete control over something I'm selling. Heh heh heh, man, you've been around. You know that."

I stepped toward him and started to raise my voice, "I've been around enough to know when someone's trying to pound sand up my ass."

Kitty started to cry and Lenny welcomed the out, picking her up in his arms and talking to her in baby talk, "Totsella, baby, did he make you cry?"

I took a few breaths and tried to calm down. I looked at Kitty and thought about the many months she'd been living with Honey, then asked, "What are you going to do with her?"

Lenny felt confident bouncing her in his arms, sensing he held all the cards. He looked at me in mock puzzlement as if he didn't know what I was talking about and said, "What's it to you?"

Frankie turned toward me and put a hand on my shoulder as if to say it was time to leave, and I spoke to Lenny for the last time I would talk to him in almost two more years, "You're right, Lenny, what the hell is it to me anyhow," and left.

Chapter 9
RUNAWAY

'Runaway' is a term that was born during that time when the Hollywood film unions or guilds had reached their zenith as closed shops rife with nepotism and featherbedding, and the subsequent inflation of film production costs caused many new or independent producers to 'run away' to a more sane economic environment out of Hollywood, out of state, or out of the country to make their films out of the strangling influence of the unions.

The original Hollywood tycoons carved out an industry with potentials far exceeding their abilities as dreamers or bookkeepers, and, in the ensuing flood of wealth they enjoyed at the expense of a growing number of artists and artisans, the disparity between the grossly ostentatious 'haves' and the dollar-a-day as an extra 'have-nots' understandably gave birth to the unions.

That army of have-nots in turn became an empire of unions slicing themselves such huge pieces of pie from the industry that two things happened. For one, management no longer had endless capital to survive the trials and experiments of creating a new art form, to explore new techniques in sets and lighting and camera trickery, to risk subjects that were offbeat, controversial, or bizarre.

The second result was in making guild work so lucrative that they all became closed shops, the resulting nepotism causing a stagnation of inbreeding and repetition, sticking with the safe tried and true subjects and treatments. Evidence of how far out of line the unions were, and also how much they've returned to reality, is to note the relatively small increase in their salary scale over the last twenty years compared to the nation's. Back when Lenny made $125 a week as a nightclub comedian, and I made $75 a week as a salesman at Lloyd's Camera Exchange, scale for director of photography was $440 a week and the lowly film loader who performed only one simple repetitious task got $225. Yet I was expected to show the entire crew every facet of any equipment they bought, and if it was something radically new, I usually took it out and worked professionally with it prior to that, but non-union.

And thereby hangs the tale (or is it tail), because when the union tail began to wag the great shaggy dog of the Hollywood studios, many producers amputated the problem by simply leaving the immediate influence of Hollywood and hiring non-union crew like myself. We worked for 50% to 75% of scale, didn't get into petty hassles because a prop man moved a gaffer's line or a gaffer's grip pushed a camera dolly, and many of us had our own equipment which, even when we were paid rental on it, precluded a whole set of planning logistics for small or short productions.

I gave up my Hollywood studio, sold my 8" x 10" view camera, my 4" x 5" press camera, my 2 1/4" x 2 1/4" single lens reflex camera, the darkroom equipment, the lighting equipment, the office equipment, and bought myself a set of fully outfitted 16mm and 35mm Arriflex motion picture cameras, my favorites among the great variety of rental cameras I had used working for Lenny.

As a 'glamor' photographer, I was offered a lot of porno film work, but, aside from the fact that it was highly illegal then, I believed in the quality of my film making abilities and didn't want to limit my work with the label 'pornographer.' Not that I was in any way a snob or puritan about pornography, having viewed its worst and appreciated its best from the ancient Greek murals illustrated in the family library books of my childhood to the 16mm two reelers of *Candy Barr* and *The Nun* I'd watched with Lenny, Frankie, and the gang.

Each time I'd rent a piece of equipment from the old Hollywood Camera Exchange, I'd think about the history of world pornography, which in this hemisphere and since the inception of photography had been suppressed in major university libraries and such places as the film vault at the Hollywood Camera Exchange, where Fred Thomas, who had supplied film makers since the inception of Hollywood, was reputed to have prints of every stag film made in Hollywood, including films of a number of superstars.

I loved to browse in the store as it was like a museum of film making, with equipment, autographed pictures, and annotated cards explaining each piece's history and what milestone films or effects it had contributed to. I'd look at the glass enclosed film vault and wonder if those old stars I saw at the Silent Movie Theater went home after seeing their legitimate films to look at illegitimate films of their youthful bodies making love.

The only film I saw from the vault was taken out by Fred for a privileged young Englishman, noticeable by his accent, who watched the old 35mm nitrate reel impassively on an old 'bulls-eye' Moviola which he left unattended when he was through. I mustered my courage and sauntered over casually to the Moviola, surreptitiously rewound the faded discolored old film, hoping the nitrate would not break or explode in its brittle instability, and viewed an authentic piece of documentary footage from, I suspect, the period of Communist Chinese expansion during the thirties. It showed three rows of Chinese peasants extending as far over the hilly countryside as the eye could see, all with hands bound behind their backs, waiting to be beheaded by three huge swordsmen who methodically and repetitiously fulfilled their function before a half dozen stoic military officials, and this grisly action continued uninterrupted for four hundred feet, almost five minutes.

I told Lenny of the incident, my anticipation of possibly seeing a famous movie star revealed sexually, and the utter turnoff it was to see the shocking horror of the film. The discussion that followed about documentary and theatrical film and television violence led to the *Captain Whackenjacker* routine based on the premise that it might be healthier for children to see sex than violence. "She looked up anxiously as his figure approached. With a curious smile on his face he slowly reached into his clothing. What ghastly weapon would he pull out? A gun? A knife? No, you guessed it, it's time for Captain Whackenjacker."

Despite my aesthetic and intellectual interest in erotica, however, I never became a pornographer. I did, however, become a freelance cinematographer on runaway film productions. I had been working on nonunion productions all along since I had my first studio on Western Avenue.

An old man named Ernie St. George had a shop around the corner on Santa Monica Boulevard and used to pay me to help him modify cine equipment for the industry. Ernie had developed one of the early wire recorders in England and other military photo equipment just before World War II. He came to the States after the war to buy surplus equipment from the U.S. government, modify it for new applications, then re-label it and sell it back to them at outrageous profits.

Ernie anticipated the advent of Techniscope, a clever wide-screen process with a fifty percent saving in film and lab costs achieved by modifying a camera to use only half the vertical dimension of the film. Ernie had done this before Technicolor patented it, by replacing the film gate of Eyemo 35mm newsreel cameras with one that had the full width of the silent frame and only half the height, then adopting the practice of reversing the exposed roll and shooting the other half of the frame in the opposite direction.   It posed complex editing problems, but probably inspired the Techniscope system, which modified not only the camera film gate but also the four perforation hole pull down claw into a two hole pull down, thereby allowing straightforward editing procedures.

Ernie eventually sold his wide screen Eyemo system to a famous retired bandleader who was transferring his investments from amusement arcades in downtown Los Angeles to a chain of soft porn movie houses for which he produced his own film product in the wide screen format. When I left Lenny, Ernie had me talk to the bandleader, who offered me the opportunity to produce his soft porn films, but I passed on it.

I learned about surplus equipment from Ernie, and, when I worked for Lloyd Berman, he had me attend the surplus auctions at nearby military bases where I'd bid on huge lots of Eyemo 35mm newsreel cameras and GSAP (gun sight aiming point) 16-mm cameras by the pound, wincing as they'd use dirt loaders to transfer hundreds of them into our rented utility trailer. Back at the store, I'd put Ernie's lessons to work, dusting them off, testing them, and cannibalizing the least of them to repair the best. They were mounted in helmets and body braces and all kinds of rigs for action shots where better cameras were too heavy, bulky, or just plain too expensive to risk.

My first freelance cinematographic work was being foolhardy enough to build and use those rigs. After I left Sam Wall, I inherited one of his former personality accounts who couldn't pay Sam's $75 a week fee. Major 'Speed' Chandler had been a balloonist in World War I, but had conned everyone who couldn't remember that far back into believing he had been an 'air ace,' as he loosely put it. He politicked his way into an executive position with Studebaker after World War II and spent his waning years in Hollywood as a lady's man, glorying in his past and eking out enough with a shaky flying school and a handful of mortgaged Piper Cubs to maintain a Beverly Hills facade. For $25 a week and expenses, I did picture stories of him teaching starlet Vikke Dugan to fly, his ten year old son dating a ten year old child actress, and the old man dating the daughters of his former girlfriends.

In 1957 he asked me if I wanted to make movies of some "damn fools" who had hired him to take them up in the air so they could jump out and see how far they would fall before being forced to use their parachutes. After talking it over, we took up two planes, one for the skydivers and another he piloted for the camera, a two-seater open cockpit plane he claimed had been his World War I fighter plane, but which was built in the twenties and bought in the forties from a retired barnstormer. I built a miniature gimble mount for the rear cockpit and had to sit so high, to allow a low center of gravity for the mount, I was almost out of the cockpit. I used Aero Ektachrome film which was the only 35mm stock I could afford as it was military surplus and, coincidentally, color balanced specifically for aerial work. Unfortunately, I could not afford to make 35mm dupe print of the exciting footage we got, and I sold the original at the first opportunity to resolve the publicity debts Speed was incurring with me. To my knowledge, it's among the earliest skydiving footage made.

In addition, there were dozens of little 'in-town runaway' assignments where I would bootleg an action or location shot for a producer saddled with a union production. I'd go to the studio, watch rushes of the scene the action shot had to tie into, and receive any associated props, wardrobe, and film stock, and sometimes a stunt person, though usually I supplied that, too. A lot of writers leaned heavily on the innate human fear of falling: the child on a bike goes over a cliff, the car goes over a cliff, the victim rolls down an embankment, the victim falls into the water. The long shot I had to tie to was usually incomplete or, in the case of a car, a piece of library footage I had to match. I usually made the POV shot (first-person point of view) with a spring wound Eyemo camera equipped with a fixed focus 25mm Eyemax lens, an excellent little war surplus optic we used to get for $25 apiece, taping the camera with styrofoam protection and strapping the assembly to a junkyard car hood mounted on two bicycles so the whole thing could be shoved off the cliff or through the flames or into the river, or whatever the script called for. If I was lucky, the equipment would survive for yet another assignment.

Some of the more interesting 'documentary' type location shots were more risky, such as shooting 'ambience' in a crowded street from a camera concealed, cameraman and all, in a coffin-sized box being wheeled through the street in a rack full of clothes. One time Bill Yee, an experimental film maker who did a beautiful documentary on Watts Towers, was driving me in his convertible through a particularly rough section of the black community of Watts when the wind whipped away the cardboard box housing I had fashioned to conceal the camera. A half dozen of the 'atmosphere' types we were photographing converged indignantly on the car, one grabbing Bill Yee by the collar as he started to accelerate, saying, "You looking for trouble, white boy?" which broke us up inasmuch as Bill is unmistakably Chinese.

These shots were bootlegged to freelancers like me because, were they shot by union crews according to union requirements, they would have cost from 10 to 100 times what we could do them for. Not only was our price lower and camera crew smaller, but we didn't require support crews for lighting, makeup, wardrobe, props, catering, security, insurance, and so on. We could get by without such support because, being a smaller crew and more resourceful than spoiled studio crews, we could work in real locations because we drew much less attention. If my stunt person broke a fingernail in a fall, that was the stunt person's problem. If I got arrested driving a car off a cliff in Malibu Canyon, that was my problem. As for the savings, the producers or directors or creative bookkeepers at the studio pocketed most of it.

After I left Lenny, Frankie felt at liberty to approach me about writing and was willing to give me total freedom with only his basic storyline to adhere to. Furthermore, knowing how discouraged I'd become doing business with Lenny, Frankie offered me a properly written contract, a $500 advance, and $500 increments upon stages of completion until the script was finished.

It was not pornography, but what used to be called a 'sexploitation' film, or what today would be considered an 'R' rated film. The original title was *Candia,* but I don't know under what name it was released. While the storyline was Frankie and his backer's private property, suffice it to say it was an amusing sex comedy that leaned heavily on our experience with 'sight material' and economizing on lip-sync production.

All this time I kept seeing Lenny's career touted during the first year of our separation. The work we had created together was considered timely, incisive social satire. Liberal West Coast critics like Herb Caen called him "brilliant" and Ralph Gleason dubbed him "Rebel With a Cause." He began to get top dollar bookings in the nation's top nightclubs, and appeared on national television. As our original routines began to wear thin, however, the newer material Lenny was performing was only occasionally based on ideas or punch lines we had originally shelved. His development of the newer material was ragged, poorly constructed, and too often the controversial subject matter was, though still valid in its premise, delivered tactlessly and offensively.

Lenny's comic talent was largely an instinctive one, born of a kind of innocent's view of the world; it was not a cultured talent, and definitely not a disciplined one. Despite the fact that he would have liked to think of himself as self made, totally independent, and 'super-hip' to the point of omnipotence, like all of us, Lenny needed help. Despite the fact that Frankie continued to be loyal to him, as he had been with Shecky, Frankie ended up working 'for' Lenny rather than 'with' Lenny. He could not adequately influence his creative work, discipline him, or save him from his drug abuse and his parasitical friends in the drug culture.

The disorientation and paranoia attendant on the drug abuse and the company he kept led Lenny to create material attacking the personal weaknesses of leading figures rather than their hypocrisies and flawed philosophies. Lawrence Welk, President Eisenhower, and Jackie Ken- nedy were made sport of for no good reason, and the conservative press took exception. After a few narcotics arrests, even though the charges didn't stick, Lenny became fair game to shoot down. When I read Walter Winchell's column dubbing Lenny "America's No. I Vomic," I literally felt sick.

Finally, I actually did run away from Hollywood, working on monster films and westerns in Tucson before the movie lot there became semi-unionized. I worked on TV action pilots in Mexico. In those days everyone was making a pilot and they were all filmed then, as videotape was in its infancy.

Frankie took a plunge into early videotape with Bill Sargent, who produced the one and only feature length 'Electronovision'' production. They used high resolution cameras and 2" video recorders, transferring the result via a kinescope setup to 35mm black and white graphic arts film that blended together the dot pattern of the high resolution monitor in the kinescope machine. The process allowed them the flexibility of three camera television production, instant playback, and all the resulting production economy. As associate producer, Frankie was largely responsible for the subject matter, a biography of Jean Harlow; Frankie was always big on biographies. The film was a boon to Carol Lynley's career, and Ginger Rogers made a comeback in it as a mature dramatic actress. Unfortunately, a concurrent production by the same name, *Harlow,* was secretly in the making and there was a big court battle over the almost simultaneous release of the two films.

Meanwhile, I worked on a runaway film in New Orleans for Dale Ireland, John Ireland's brother. It was originally titled *Hot Rain* and was finally released as *Sin Street USA.* I acted as still photographer, second unit cinematographer on an Arriflex 35mm camera, and assistant cameraman to Basil Bradbury behind a Mitchell BNC (blimped noiseless camera). The film starred Gary Clark (of *The Virginians*), Jackie Ebier, who had modeled for me several times in the past, and Jackie's former boyfriend who worked under the name Donald Herron, one of several stage names he used in the many excellent roles he did in the sixties.

I ended up doing a little of everything on that production, including procuring locations from former friends and associates, playing the guitar for Jackie when she needed some tempo for a few dance steps in a scene, and stepping in front of the camera to play a longshoreman. At one point, a local actress who was to play a hooker on the comer of Jackson Square failed to show, so I went to nearby Harry's Bar and cast the part from one of the young female customers at the bar, fortunately getting her to sign a handwritten release I drafted on the spot. Sure enough, thirty minutes after we shot the scene her lawyer boyfriend returned talking lawsuit, but the release covered us.

Basil Bradbury returned to Hollywood to complete a film with Frankie Ray, *Attack of the Star Creatures,* in which Frankie and Bobby Ball are tyrannized by giant female beauties from outer space, some of whom had danced at the Near and Far.

While in New Orleans, I heard they were going to shoot Tennessee Williams's play *This House is Condemned* in the little Gulf Coast town where I was born and raised. When I got there, Joe Pine was just doing the pre-production chores and I heard the story about how much time and money they had spent scouting for a location throughout the south to find the right combination of train station, roundhouse, bridge, and nearby community with a carpenter gothic house. When they looked all over the eastern seaboard for such a locale and failed, they asked Tennessee Williams if they could change those elements in the script, and he told them they'd find it all in this little town where he had lived and written for many years, writing the story about the very family that had lived in that carpenter gothic rooming house for railroad workers. While many in that little town might have been able to tell Joe Pine that, I was perhaps the only one in Hollywood who would have known, but I didn't move in union circles.

Being non-union precluded my getting any camera work on *This House* is *Condemned,* but I was thrown a bone as Public Liaison, which involved casting locals as extras and occasionally chauffeuring Natalie Wood and Robert Redford to their accommodations in Biloxi.

As fate seemed determined to lure me eastward, I accepted an offer to do public relations for a small hotel chain in Jamaica. It included producing their postcards and menus, establishing an ongoing PR campaign, and producing a travelogue film to be used by travel agents and tourist boards. I was headquartered in a Port Antonio hotel called Jamaica Reef, which was formerly owned by Errol Flynn and stood at the dividing point of a beautiful double harbor and directly across from Navy Island, which had been won by Flynn in a card game.

There was an attractive brunette staying there who was kept by a Texas millionaire. Her name was Mary Murray and she was the embodiment of Audrey Hepburn in her role as Holly Golightly in *Break- fast at Tiffany's*. I had always had the hots for Audrey Hepburn and this was the nearest I seemed likely to come to the fulfillment of a longtime fantasy. The hotel owned a beautiful Chris Craft yacht that no one was responsible for and could be seen slowly sinking at the dock down by Flynn's Inn. I took it upon myself to confiscate the boat as my private haunt, pumping out the bilges daily to keep it afloat and sitting up on the flying bridge with my portable typewriter.

Mary accosted me brazenly her third day there, as Holly Golightly should, climbing aboard my private domain in an almost nonexistent knit bikini and audaciously daring to criticize the piece I was writing, a short story about a jet-setter I knew in Paris. Mary posed and twisted her sinewy limbs before me like a cat playing with a mouse for hours until sunset when, under the cover of gathering darkness, I grabbed her by the arm and half dragged her to the cabin below. She made the barest pretenses of resisting, her expression vacillating between mock horror and squealing glee. She thoroughly loved the strength and vengeance I wreaked on her trim but solid frame in retaliation for the hours of taunting she subjected me to. Ultimately, she wanted to test every bunk in the huge yacht, those that rocked this way with the boat and those that rocked that way with the boat, challenging me to find positions and techniques to accommodate them.

She joined me most afternoons on the flying bridge, telling me stories of her childhood in an orphanage and the adventures of her young life, some of which I believed and a few of which I wrote short stories about. She came to me every single night, entering unannounced and wordlessly initiating lovemaking like an addict thirsting for a drug that required searching every nook and cranny, and which always left her with the most satiated expression on her face like a wily and well fed cat.

She always liked to court mini-dangers like losing a head on challenge with a billygoat that sent her tumbling head over heels down a hill, trying to get dressed and back to her room before the Texan arrived, and standing stark naked on the rooftop outside my window facing the port to wave goodbye to the delighted passengers of the weekly cruise ship as it departed in the night.

She seemed to want to pack all of life she could into the shortest time she could. Finally, the Texan moved her to other quarters, and I'm told she left bitterly but fatalistically, without saying goodbye to me.

I saw her a month later happily dancing the Jamaican dance called the 'Jump Up' in a local club with some French sailors off a sailing vessel. I cut in on her and, while the two of us bounced up and down foolishly to the music, I said, "Why?"

She flashed her Holly Golightly smile, "Because I have to keep moving."

I grimaced, "But with that Texan?"

Her smile brightened, "But I don't love him," and she jumped even higher.

I automatically tried to match her elevations, "Why can't you love me?"

Her jumping became strained, "Who said I don't?"

I stopped jumping, "Then why?"

She looked down at the floor and slowed to a jog, "I haven't got time."

I grabbed her by the shoulders to stop her. "I don't believe you."

She lifted tear filled eyes to me and stammered, "I wish I didn't have to believe me either," and tore herself away, running through the confused sailors and out of sight.

I returned from paradise to a smoggy civilization with a bag full of songs, poems, short stories, and screenplays, and had the funny feeling of having lived through yet another whole lifetime apart from Hollywood, apart from Korea, and apart from my 'flaming youth' in the French Quarter.

Chapter 10
WORDS AND NUMBERS

I make no apologies for being a dreamer and a philosopher. I regard it as no special merit nor shame, believing that anyone who discovers they do not necessarily have to see themselves or live their lives by others' values, the church's or state's or Madison Avenue's, has reached the threshold of being a philosopher. It follows that, supplanting other's preconceived values, one has to evolve one's own philosophy.

We weave our philosophies with words, and the semantic ambiguities in these tapestries can turn our vision of perfection into a nightmare of perversion. The pen is mightier than the sword is true in both a negative as well as a positive sense. A tyrant can pen *Mein Kampf* while sitting in prison, but a prophet can also pen *Hitler and the MCA* while sitting in prison on an obscenity charge, trying to remind people that it's the Madison Avenue mentality that created tyrants like 'der Fuhrer.' Words are not the villains, rather the unwillingness of the listener to understand how they operate, to apply the logic that would reveal the plausibility or implausibility of a statement. Ignorance is in the ear of the listener, usually a lazy listener who wants to be spoon fed oversimplifications.

Because words beg to be abused, science invented numbers early in the game, science probably being some clever caveman shaman who invented the digital system we have today by observing that all of his species to whom he wanted to communicate a numerical concept had ten digits on their hands. What strange and perhaps superior potentials do spiders and octopuses have with a digital system of eight, and consider the centipede who grows new digits at will.

But we homo sapiens have done some laudable things with our handful of ten digits system. We've applied it not only to quantities, but to express two dimensions, three dimensions, and some abstract concepts which words find difficult to communicate.

I have adopted certain numerical expressions with which I try to convey to people that I do not presume to judge right or wrong, but rather the degree to which I agree or disagree. Basically, I come to terms with many things by basing them on a scale of one to a hundred, or visualizing them on a 360-degree circle. If something is more than 50% positive, or its aim falls from one side of the circle into the other 180 degrees of the goal side, it's worthy of consideration, the difference between consideration, endorsement, participation, and passionate merger being subject to each individual's choice of values. I'm conservative enough, or perhaps experienced enough, to reserve endorsement for a score of 75% positive, participation 85%, and passion somewhere over 95%. But, by the same token, I'm likely to be more generous or objective than most in scoring more things in the 50% region worthy of consideration.

For a person who makes a living with words and images, I had to resort to my numerical parameters one night when Sally called me asking me to come back to work for Lenny. The words that might express my feelings pro and con were too emotional, too painful, and too confusing.

I had worked for almost three years with Lenny, helping him transcend obscurity for international fame and fortune, with little or no recompense or recognition for myself. I had been separated from him for almost two years, during which time I had enjoyed more money, travel, women, recognition, and film making than I ever

148

had with Lenny. Also during those two years, I had witnessed from a distance the methodic self-destruction Lenny had wreaked on himself and the projects in which Frankie and I had invested our hopes and talents so heavily, and I felt a mingled pain and resentment such as one might feel for an alcoholic spouse.

Sally said Lenny needed me because his autobiography was floundering. I knew Lenny was floundering in a sea of self indulgence which required some external discipline to overcome. But I also knew that I would not see any compensation because of the coterie of junkies that surrounded him, and any recognition would not win against Lenny's. ego. I declined.

Sally, however, was always shrewd, and, like her son, an innate psychologist. She knew better than anyone, perhaps better than Lenny and I, the conflicts which separated us. She said, "Listen to me now. The baby's not in Europe with Honey any more, the baby's with me. Lenny gave Kitty to me. He knew that situation couldn't go on. Kitty's with me. You can stop by and see her on your way to Lenny;s. You gotta go up there! He's up to his ass in pages of transcript and hookers and all that shit, and he's gonna blow what may be his last chance to get his shit together."

"Did Lenny ask you to call me?" I asked, wondering how much I sounded like an estranged girlfriend who was being invited back.

"Time and time again. For months now I've been calling that schvartza agency you were working for and they kept shining me on with some story that you were out of the country. I figured you were still pissed with Lenny and didn't wanna see him."

As much as I loved her, I never knew when I could totally believe Sally, but she was probably telling the truth because Lenny had more need for me than I of him at that point. As long as it didn't require any public acknowledgment, Lenny was shameless in what he would say or do to get what he wanted in a one-to-one relationship. I did, however, go by Sally's to assure myself that Kitty was safely in her custody, which was the factor that swung my decision to work with Lenny again back into the 85% region.

Sally's description was not the least exaggerated, as I found when I stepped into Lenny's downstairs bedroom. He was on his hands and knees searching through a sea of photocopied court transcripts that literally covered the entire carpeting up to his terrycloth robed tush. Replaying the tape in my brain of that moment he saw me does not distort or diminish the expression on his face which, if it did not contain some element of love, was at the very least happy relief. The beatific expression broadened to a wide eyed grin as he stumbled through the sea of paper to hug me, saying, "William, William, where have you been? You're just the man I need. Now we can get something done."

I returned the hug and relished the moment briefly for whatever warmth or sincerity it might hold. Then, more to establish a working discipline than to milk one of the rare moments where I had the upper hand with Lenny, I held him slightly apart from me and asked, "Did you ask Sally to call me?"

He turned into the room and started picking up papers. "Yeah, yeah, didn't she tell you I'm writing my book?"

I continued in a monotone, "Did you talk to her since she phoned me?"

Lenny brusquely focused his attention on the three other people in the room, his houseman, John Judnich, and two scantily clad girls. "You guys go fix something to eat, go do something in the other room, just go, okay, you guys." When they had left, he began snuffling as he looked down at the papers he shuffled in his hands, then looked up unsmiling at me and said, "I need you, Bill. I don't have much money, but I need you." He let the papers trail to the floor as his arms hung limply at his sides. "You can see that, can't you? I need you."

I looked out the picture window at the predawn gray of the Los Angeles skyline and said, "Before I leave today, I expect you to talk in realistic terms about paying me. Before I start, I want to be reassured I have complete authority which shall be superseded by you only when I say your head is straight. Otherwise I don't see..."

The ecstatic smile returned to his face and he grabbed both my hands, interrupting me with "You got it, you got it!" Then he did a line from Lord Buckley's *The Naz* routine, "You lay it down, sweet double-hipness, whomp, and we'll pick it up."

And, as Lord Buckley would say, I llllllaid it.

For starters, I asked everyone who was not salaried to leave, which caused the redhead to disappear. The brunette wasn't salaried, but she was a good soldier and stayed, even after I asked her to change out of her baby doll nightie into some slacks and a shirt.

I busied everyone stacking the paperwork in neat piles against one wall, then transferring it to stacks against the opposite wall separated by case file numbers which I started to list numerically on the wall with labels that could be removed later. Lenny, in his eager haste, started scribbling the numbers on the wall with a marker, but mostly out of sequence.

Once that was in progress, I took Lenny in the other room and asked him about the manuscript.

"Well, I had this girl typing the manuscript, see, but a week or so ago I got horny and I jumped her. Now she thinks she's in love with me. She says she's coming over to work, but all she does when she gets here is cry because the other broads are here and all. I dunno, I always manage to screw things up somehow."

There was no manuscript. Bits of it were being held for ransom by unpaid secretaries and at least one lovesick one who only showed up to do melodramatic suicide routines. I finally had to get file copies back from *Playboy* of the few completed installments they had as a basis to get a handle on the book.

When I left Lenny two years before, I had sent him every photograph, every negative, every page of everything I had ever done for him, all beautifully organized and filed in books, binders, and boxes. At the beginning of our separation, I saw those materials used in publicity, in records, and in the later routines where only a seed of my contribution remained recognizable.

When I returned to Lenny, not one scrap of those materials or organization remained to be seen. The files, the audio control room, and the house were in a shambles. Lenny himself did not look as sleek or as healthy as he did two years before.

I took a bread and butter job in cinema equipment sales with Bob Gamble's Photo Supply because, not only did my work with Lenny not begin to provide a living, I also needed to replenish my cinema and audio equipment and it didn't hurt to be next to the wholesale sources. It also didn't hurt my efforts to re-establish the audio room in Lenny's house where my original installation of racked tape decks, custom built mini console, and laboriously wired patch bay that fed from all parts of the house was now just so many pounds of badly damaged spare parts.

In bits and spurts, whenever money could be spared from Lenny's legal fees and other needs, I tediously rebuilt the audio room which was to become the heart of Lenny's subsequent creative works. Lenny had been introduced to drugs long before I met him, but, from our earliest association, I was responsible for making him, as one reporter put it, a "tape recorder junkie."

I tried to use recorders in writing with Frankie and

originally with Lenny, particularly since neither of them typed or were particularly good grammarians, but it proved pointless because the principal reason they collaborated with me was so I could ride herd over their wandering imaginations and discipline the material into some semblance of the intended plot. Giving them a recorder to work with when I wasn't around largely inhibited them and, at the most, produced a lot of unrelated ramblings that offered little more than working from a dictionary or a telephone book. They both needed the interaction of bouncing ideas off someone, and I was, at the very least, a someone capable of evaluating and developing those ideas, and sometimes more.

After the first album had to be recorded live in the nightclub before an audience because Lenny couldn't perform in a cold impersonal sound studio, he got used to recording most of his performances for the creative advantages of reviewing his stage presence and ad-lib material for further development. But this was all still dependent upon a live audience to get anything out of Lenny and onto tape.

Lenny began to really take an interest in tape recorders when I was working as an investigator and his latent voyeurism was titillated by the 'eavesdropping' element in my work. He had been around jazz musicians who were audiophiles and, while he never really understood the technology of audio electronics, he was enamored of sophisticated audio equipment because of that association. But. when it came to the tape recorder as a 'bugging' device, he suddenly developed a passion to understand, equip himself, and employ recorders offstage for the first time as a 'technology of titillation.'

When I began working on the autobiography with him, the unstable money and environmental situation precluded hiring a typist, so conditioning Lenny to use tape recorders for dictation was the only way to go. I established a system of taking the reels of dictation myself, when there was money, to a typist and providing one typed copy for Lenny, one for *Playboy,* and one for me, because Lenny's copy would invariably be lost within a day or two and he'd need photocopies of mine.

Some people will find it curious that a performer who stood with a microphone before huge audiences most of his life could get 'mike fright' when placed alone in a room with the same mike, but Lenny, not unlike others I've known in similar situations, did just that. It's rather like going to a shrink for the first time. It's one thing to talk about your intimate life to either a friend, or an audience of a thousand if you have a performer's talent and temperament, but it's an entirely different thing to tell your life story to a cold, impersonal machine.

I can see his nervous face before me as I listen to that first tape I made him make in the newly reconstructed audio room back in 1961. With my voice in the background explaining the layout of the new console, he starts in a subdued voice, "Hello, one, one, one, one, one. Dear Mr. Thomas, I'm a comedian that ... works on the principle of reporting. I report, er, about everything I see during the day, my own personal life ... in a way that, eh ... It's very strange, I find myself inhibited by the microphone."

Economic and professional desperation helped force him to discipline himself to many hours of daily tape dictation and, with John Judnich's help, the tapes conformed to my system of color-coded leaders, labels, reels, and boxes to help me categorize and minimize my editing of them. For the most part, Lenny accepted my procedural dictates and allowed John to apply the leaders and so forth. What Lenny didn't know was that John and I had a secret code, yellow leader to indicate incomprehensible garbage. Much later, when I dutifully went through the 'yellow garbage' looking for lost items,

I didn't find anything that was pertinent to the book, but I did find some fascinating tidbits that were indicative of Lenny's earlier fascination with my investigative techniques. John Judnich was a boon to Lenny. John was a rehabilitated junkie who at least understood where Lenny was coming from, but John apparently had his act together well enough to help Lenny try to hold onto his. John had been a boatbuilder in San Francisco and was talented with his hands, always working on some redecorating project for Lenny. He chauffeured Lenny, cooked or catered from a deli, and, most of all, protected Lenny when he was incapacitated, which became an increasing amount of the time. John and I got along pretty well and commiserated with each other when Lenny got really whacko and there was no rhyme or reason up at the house.

I required Lenny to pay me 50% of my salary for my services as editor, photographer, audio engineer, or whatever, accepting a verbal agreement that some day, when his hassles were over, he'd make up the deficit to me. I had tired of written agreements which sat in my files as constant reminders of unfulfilled promises, and I had accepted the evolution of my role from collaborator to editor, film co-producer to cinematographer, and so forth. Still, he would occasionally give me rubber checks, or I would get a glimpse of him investing ten times as much as his stipend to me for his purely personal indulgences which did him increasing harm.

There was little opportunity to contribute to the writing of the book.

An autobiography is, after all, a first-person narrative, and Lenny's personality, as well as his chronic inability to concentrate for long, precluded making any permanent or serious input in that respect. The most I could hope to do was edit the chronology, dust off the worst of the grammatical errors, and try to organize the writing while keeping Lenny on an even keel. This period was perhaps the most difficult test of the curious relationship Lenny and I had. Lenny's emotions were mixed, to say the least. He felt a sense of guilt for the unfulfilled promises and obligations to me, an unnecessary sense of rejection because of my disdain for drugs, a competitiveness because my long and integral creative contributions challenged his egocentric desire to appear totally original and self-made, and an insecurity because of my more cultured background. On the other hand, he felt positive emotions for me which, for the first time since the initial flush when we began working together four years before, he openly expressed to me.

For about two months after I returned, he had the habit of meeting me at the gate when I arrived, of touching or gripping my arm when he'd say, "Now dig, here's how we'll do it," and saying to me at odd moments when he'd awake to see me there or we'd finish a long grind of work, "Gee, man, I'm really glad to see you back."

One small tribute to me was expressed silently. I had returned from Jamaica with a full beard, neatly trimmed after the fashion of Sir Girwain in the *Prince Valiant* comic strip I admired in my childhood. I had noticed that, as heroic as Prince Valiant was, Sir Girwain always ended up with the ladies, and I somehow felt that the Mephistophelian triple peak to his beard line had something to do with his charisma, and I adopted its fashion. Within a few weeks of my return, Lenny grew a beard for the first time since he I had known him. Lenny's new beard had my triple peak line to it, which he achieved by watching me shave daily with avid curiosity and asking my advice in trimming it overzealously. Despite the excessive trimming that made it take three times as long as necessary to mature, his new beard developed into a handsome, luxuriant growth that helped hide some of the fullness his face was acquiring and gave him a more messianic image than ever before. After all, it was also the beard line Western painters had put on their interpretations of Christ for centuries, but here it adorned the face of a dark handsome Jew with sparkling eyes and a prophet's tongue.

In writing his autobiography, Lenny could look back nostalgically to his childhood on the East Coast, and forward to the possible implications of his legal crusade, but he could not see the present in perspective. He could not sense, or feel it pertinent to reveal, those elements and experiences which had been critical in his transformation from obscurity to international recognition. He glossed over lightly the years between childhood sexual discoveries and religious con games in Florida to being 'discovered' by the famous, who found him in the nation's leading nightclubs and served on the silver platter of a record album. As Kenneth Tynan said in the foreword of Lenny's autobiography, "In the years that followed, it was not Bruce but my friends that improved. One by one they began to discover that they had always admired him." And, as the famous came around one by one to admire Lenny, he began to forget one by one the years and people who helped lift him from obscurity to the leading nightclubs and record industry where he was 'discovered.'

As the book began to shape up, I suggested to. Lenny that it might be more realistic and inspiring to hear him acknowledge moments of recognition, evolution, and redirection in his career, to know that he had shared and respected the creative talents of others, and that he was not born super-hip, that there was the slightest glimmer of humility in him. But it seemed his concept of the book was that the message of the comedy material and the court cases was paramount, and anything in between had to be ribald anecdotes.

I subverted my emotions about Lenny to my numerical parameters.

I was, in fact, resentful of Lenny's dishonesty and

157

exploitation of me, envious of the opportunities success had offered and he had wasted, and hurt that he would not publicly acknowledge and recognize Frankie's or my contribution. On the other hand, I had come to share Frankie's appreciation of Lenny's dynamic performing talents, his ability to lure an audience into his confidence where they would accept his radical approach to otherwise highly personal subjects, and the tenaciousness with which he pursued these themes in the face of being targeted for rebuke by the establishment.

But emotions, like words, are fickle, ambiguous things, easily abused, twisted, and misunderstood. As Lenny said on one of those garbage tapes I now sometimes listen to, talking in a letter to one of his lawyers about his routines being misquoted in court and used as evidence against him, "Words changed a bit can bring a bitter change." Lenny's behavior was sometimes less than 50% acceptable, but the truth of his philosophy and the sincerity of my love for him was always 95% plus.

Chapter 11
BLACK AND WHITE

I've always been fascinated with the effect black and white have on people. People are affected by the frequency of colors, and some relate red with anger, blue with depression, yellow with happiness, green with envy, and pink with lust. But what about black and white?

Black and white are the two polarized visual absolutes and we can use them both in profound and constructive ways, blending black with colors to make them somber and dramatic, and blending white with colors to make them joyous and brilliant. Frequently we juxtapose black and white to emphasize a statement by their contrast.

I once stood in the middle of a huge explosion and saw the most total white and, later in the hospital, experienced the most total blackness one can comprehend in this life. No choice of words I can convey to you would describe the totality of those two absolutes I saw. But, hopefully, these pages might help you understand the influence such absolutes have on us all.

When, in later years, I taught photography, I'd always have a student start with black and white film because there are things one can see in black and white that can't be seen in color, or not as easily. I believe you have to learn black and white first before you can do anything creatively with color. Jumping into color first is like trying to play Beethoven with only a knowledge of the scale, but an ignorance of timing and phrasing and shading. If you took a color photograph and removed the black and white from it, it would have no dimension, no separation, no feeling of life or reality to it.

You might think that if you compared a color photograph to an identical black and white one, the black and white might be lacking, but not necessarily so. While there are some subtleties that color expresses best, black and white can stand alone to express the basic premise, the plot of a picture, sometimes more emphatically than color, a plot which may even be hidden in color.

People are not black and white, even when they say they are. I myself am pink and tan with a little bit of red, brown, and yellow around the edges. Most people who say they are 'black' are usually some kind of brown or tan with occasional red, yellow, and blue tinges. You can paint some Polish people brown and they'd look appropriate in Nigeria, paint some Nigerians tan and send them to a Navajo reservation, and some Navajos yellow and send them to China. They might look 'appropriate' in a snapshot with their new paint job and cultural background, but there the simile stops, because what we are is not determined by that one millimeter of flesh that covers our exterior, except, unfortunately, in the eyes of most others.

When it comes to people, the underlying black and white absolutes that determine their timing, their dimension, and their basic premise is not discernible in their complexion and is not as obvious as a black and white photo or the printed words on this page. Finding those absolutes requires peeling away all the layers of color painted on by years of conditioning; both ours and theirs.

Lenny and I, partly because of the wisdom of our single parent mothers, had mostly escaped from the inhibition of living up or down to whatever image others saw in us, and, consequently, were better prepared to accept each individual according to his or her behavior rather than an easily stereotyped external image. Raised in New York City, Lenny had been somewhat cloistered from intimate contact with some ethnic groups. He only began to discover and explore them as exotica around the time I first met him, often with the innocence, awkwardness, and sometimes unwitting offensiveness a child displays when he mimics an oriental's eyes or tries to see if the 'black' will rub off someone's skin. Lenny never intentionally hurt anyone in that context, and his few faux pas I witnessed crushed him with guilt when he realized his query had been misunderstood or his humor inappropriate.

The few blacks he had been close to were jazz musicians with a sophistication and drug culture camaraderie that led him to make the same mistake of many non-blacks who thought that, because "some of their best friends were black," they understood the 'black experience' which, in reality, is as large and diverse a complex of attitudes and subcultures as any other ethnic group.

Lenny later confessed that when he first met me he dismissed me as a 'redneck,' remembering his only auto trip across the South primarily with the image of two bullies in a pickup truck who harassed the 'New York Jew' in the Cadillac. But the exceptional thing about Lenny was that his mind was not closed, and his perception allowed him to appreciate the quality of the work I did with Frankie and to share our adventures together both professionally and personally.

When it came to other cultures, however, some of those adventures were vicarious, as Lenny continued to live in an environment isolated more and more by the drug culture and police harassment.

Case in point. Jackie Gale (in later years you saw him in *Tin Men* with Danny DeVito and Richard Dreyfuss) had been a drummer with a backup group Sally worked with in New York. When he hit the West Coast in the late 1950s, he knew no one but Sally. She was subbing for Frankie at the Near and Far while Frankie was on the road with Lenny and I was still at Cosmo Alley, both clubs closing with thousands of others at 2AM, as required by the California liquor licensing laws. After closing, Sally asked me to "show Jackie around." But where do you, as Jackie put it, "find some action" after two in the morning?

Though Jackie was about my age and we got along great, he was not exactly the 'coffeehouse' type, and if I'd taken him to the no-alcohol all night coffeehouses like Xanadu near the LACC campus or the dozens which existed in Venice then, he would surely have been taken for the 'fuzz' in his natty 'uptown' attire which called for a tinkling glass of booze in his hand to go along with his particular repartee.

In order to fill that hand with its tinkling glass, I suggested going to a black 'after hours' club I knew, operated by one of the lesser but notable luminaries of the boxing world on the South side of town. After cautioning him not to use some of the terminology in his affirmative response about "schvartsa girls," we were on our way.

Jackie loved the place, from the scary ride getting there through Watts to the interior of what seemed like a quiet residence on the outside, but throbbed inside with colored lights, recorded music played forty decibels too loud, and the walls completely lined with dime store framed autographed 8 x 10 glossies of every fight personality known with a celebrity's arm draped around them.

After a series of introductions, I met a cherubic little girl who agreed to introduce Jackie to someone who turned out to be an equally attractive lady. It wasn't until we got the two ladies back to Jackie's apartment off Sunset Strip that we discovered my date was the daughter of his date.

Lenny loved the story of Jackie Gale ending up with the black mother of my little black cherub, in part because the principals and the setting were in keeping with his primary reference point on the black community. He felt safe with the image of the 'Kingfish' and all the black hookers, but was uneasy in any straight black society, and all the more so among cultured blacks.

When I went to work for California's leading black public relations firm and produced films and publications for their major clients, Lenny's only interest was if any of the models wanted to meet him. When we worked on the publicity for the premiere of the play, *Amen Corners,* and I had the privilege of occasional long and intimate conversations with James Baldwin at the Mayfair apartment he always kept in Hollywood, I asked Jimmy if he'd like to meet Lenny and he said yes, but Lenny declined. When Bob DeCoy shared his then unpublished manuscripts, *Black Genesis* and *Negritian History* with me, I tried to relay to Lenny those parts I thought were so parallel to his views, but Lenny was indifferent.

Even closer to his own genre, when Redd Foxx took over what used to be the Slate Brother's Club, his then current girlfriend modeled for me, and so I was in direct contact with Redd. Knowing Lenny's temerity regarding blacks, I approached Lenny first with the idea of his making a triumphal return to that club as the first white to play there under the new management and with a largely civil rights theme to his material. He flatly refused.

Lenny had his own token black, Eric Miller, a jazz guitarist steeped in the drug culture who, ironically, strongly resembled James Baldwin in looks. Eric lived with Lenny intermittently and performed in some of Lenny's civil rights routines which I had no part in writing. They were sometimes based on vague ideas or solid punch lines to things we had collaborated on and shelved, but I considered those routines with Eric among the most contrived and awkward of Lenny's work.

Lenny accused me of having a penchant for black women because of my southern background. "You crackers see all that shiny black ass all around you and can't touch it because it's taboo. Then, as soon as you cross the Mason Dixon line, whammo, you dive in where Yankees fear to tread."

In response, I asked him if he'd rather be stuck on a desert island with Sophie Tucker or Cicely Tyson. His reply was, "Who's Cicely Tyson," which was a fair question as she had at that time only done one film with Sammy Davis, but she was my conception of 'black is beautiful.' I said, "Okay, forget that. Would you rather be stuck on a desert island with Sophie Tucker or Lena Horne?"

He shrugged, "Okay, you made your point. But so far they haven't put me on a desert island, I haven't made it with Lena Home, and I still say you got a thing for black chicks." My 'desert isle' defense ended up as a capper to one of Lenny's civil rights routines.

However, that didn't slow Lenny down if I brought a black model up to shoot a layout at his house with the view, the pool, and the mirrored rooms. He'd loiter around surreptitiously, then ask if they'd like to stay to dinner and say he'd see to it they got home later, but I'd always take them home after the photography more for fear of exposing them to drugs than to his lechery.

Lenny was always interested in attractive women if they were hookers, looked or behaved like hookers, or would let him treat them like hookers. Lenny sensed that straight black women were the last of any group that would let a man treat them like a hooker. Whether by tradition or experience, they had enough of being impersonally ordered to do things, then casually dismissed, and the last person they appreciated it from was some white man masking his insecurity. Lenny had many such insecurities, and he found black women too challenging to include any that I know of in his company.

However, Lenny was not a bigot; rather, he was culturally insulated. He started out as a curious, uninhibited, possibly even amoral child, and, in the course of his writing and comedy exploration, became what I would consider a sociologist of sorts, who believed more in the whole of society than in any of its separate political, religious, or ethnic parts. Like myself, Lenny was not a joiner, belonged to no social, professional, or activist organizations. He held his American Guild of Variety Artists card out of necessity and that was it.

Civil rights was an issue which, like many people, Lenny essentially agreed with, but felt reached some conflicting if not ridiculous separatist and semantic extremes. It was a period when preferential treatment in substandard scholastic evaluations was defined as "our way of becoming equal," and such words as anthropology, race, Negro, and colored became dirty words. Militant groups sought a separate black state within the continental limits and put equal fervor into movements to capitalize the word 'black.'

Lenny gave wide berth to any act or verbalization that would identify him with any organized ideology. In the prologue of *Show Biz Heaven* he says, "I am not a moral person," with which the vast majority of his audiences would disagree, but Lenny shied away self consciously from anything that bespoke morality, ideology, spirituality, or commitment. He felt those terms and postures had been abused enough to warrant cynicism, if not actual scorn, and maybe even a few well aimed rotten tomatoes.

I was totally in accord with him years before when he played head trips on the clergyman who tried to chase our film crew off the street comer in front of his church. There was one moment, however, in the last few years when I felt embarrassed by his overt disdain for a religious individual, even though it was the chemicals in his veins that caused his behavior.

I was doing mix downs in the audio control room

at his house, seeing Lenny grow more hyper by the minute as he was in the peak of one of his drug cycles. Lenny shot 'speed' (methadrine) for which he had a doctor's prescription as a legitimate drug to counteract narcolepsy, although I never saw evidence that he was so afflicted. Lenny would start out a cycle completely straight and dried out, function with fair efficiency for three or four weeks, show increasingly noticeable deterioration of his physical and mental capacities for five or six weeks, during which he rarely slept and began eating in a haphazard fashion or not at all, and finally hit a two-week peak when he could not concentrate for more than a few minutes on a single subject, concoct bizarre schemes to install an astronomical telescope over his bed or mine the driveway, and finally sleep fitfully sixteen to twenty hours a day until he dried out enough to start the cycle all over again.

I had retreated into the control room because Lenny had become so bizarre he was almost incomprehensible, and I found it painful to witness. Someone brought an American Indian up to the house, a handsome, imposing man in face and figure with a beautiful, sonorous voice. I think it was the man's attire that first incited Lenny's ridicule. The man had a feathered hat, plaid shirt, khaki pants, and a leather bag amulet hung around his neck on a leather thong. He looked like a healthy forty, but said he was in his late sixties, and struck a mischievous gleam in Lenny's eye when he announced he was a chief and a medicine man from a joint collection of Califomia tribes. Lenny began to mock the man almost immediately by snidely emphasizing the title 'Chief.' "Well hello, *Chief.* Never met a real *Chief.* John, get the *Chief* something to eat. Tell me, what does a *Chief* eat? We're all out of bear, coyote, and pine cones, *Chief.*"

The man told Lenny that he had never heard of him until three days prior when "the spirits" had instructed him during meditation to seek Lenny out, to "witness" him (which he had done by attending Lenny's performance earlier that evening), and to inform him that he was on the right track and to "persevere," which, with Lenny's notoriety at the time, might not have been a difficult analysis to make, but a very practical and positive one nonetheless.

The man had been unable to contact Lenny at the club, but had been brought up after the last show by one of Lenny's hangers-on who, after the man's brief statement, began to talk as if the man had left or was an animated robot from the start. "Didn't I tell you I had a kooky surprise for you, Len, baby? Ain't he a gas, and he's for real, baby. Look at that face, right off a nickel."

Lenny was in a euphoria compounded by the idolatry of the two or three hero worshipers who were always around him at this stage of his cycle. I expected no more from the parasite who had brought the man in and talked about him like he was a toy he'd bought for Lenny, but I was appalled when Lenny began to talk about the man in the same way, neither acknowledging what the man said nor his very existence as a human.

I had been drawn into the room by the sound of the man's voice, and now I felt compelled to apologize to him, but he raised his hand to interrupt my apology and say, "Don't worry, I know Lenny isn't here right now, but, when he comes back, tell him what I've said." I talked to the man for half an hour about his travels and lectures through the community of California tribes he served, had tea with him on the patio, and wondered if he was a talented bullshitter who had some con he would eventually try to work on us, or if he was for real. When I offered to drive him back to town he declined, saying he would enjoy the walk of miles down from the Hollywood Hills because, "There is still some life in these hills that I need to breathe before I return to town." As he left he added, "Remember to tell Lenny what I said."

Two weeks later when I told Lenny what the man said, Lenny blinked and stared at me perplexed, trying vainly to remember the incident, then laughed self-consciously and changed the subject.

Film projects with Lenny had also bogged down. By this time 1 had produced several 16mm 'industrial films,' as they're called, and made enough in public relations and other fields to risk investing in small 16mm productions over which 1 had sufficient control to keep them from going astray. I asked Lenny to let me produce an animated film based on several of his routines 1 felt would lend themselves to such vignettes, but he flatly refused. Much later he would allow someone to try the idea with *The Masked Man*, but the experience was neither profitable nor satisfying to him. When he cited the incident to me as proof that my previous idea wouldn't have worked, 1 reminded him of his routine about being busted because a vice officer did his act before a grand jury and Lenny had complained, "I got busted for his act."

1 wanted to do film work that would be both artistically creative and socially constructive. Working in the black community, I had been working with the civil rights issue with black and white leaders in industry, labor, politics, and at the grass-roots level from community groups to the underground. Rather than propaganda films to continually exhort adults with preconceived and crystallized attitudes, I felt the most needed product at that time were better educational films for very young black children who had not yet become cynical and apathetic.

I researched available films and decided that what was intended as 'inspiring' films for black children delivered two crippling messages: (1) there was no room for great black leadership except in the midst of revolution, as all black heroes of films at that time were from the Civil War period, and (2) the only success for contemporary blacks was in the fields of sports and entertainment, and

168

who needs an education to hit a ball or sing and dance.

I designed a proposal for an educational series that could be used both in elementary schools and also in the hope of commercial TV dissemination, as PBS was not a reality then. I chose thirteen living black Americans who were at the height of recognition for their accomplishments in America in every field *but* sports and entertainment: an astronaut, a scientist, an opera singer, the head of a multi-million dollar industry, a general, a writer, a chief of a metropolitan police department, a sculptor, a heart surgeon, a ballet master, a journalist, and a classical composer; half in the fine arts and half in the 'real' world.

I scripted the pilot on the sculptor, whose works grace museums throughout the world. His life and work was a visual subject that would be less costly to film for many reasons. In vain, I sought backing from the black community, but got a lot of requests from very wealthy black entertainers and politicians to, "See if you can get me a good buy on one of his works while you're there." White industry simply said, "I don't much give a damn about the film, but if you were black we could write it off in a minute as equal opportunity hogwash."

I sold everything but the equipment I needed to make the film and raised $5,000 to take with me to Jamaica where the sculptor lived. I had contacts with the Jamaican Film Board, the Jamaican Library Service, and the University of the West Indies, because I had the foresight to protect myself from hassles about work permits this time. I also had the loan of a friend's car and house on the north coast close to where my subject lived.

The sculptor, Richmond Barthe, first interested me because his work is not super modern or abstract, and I confess I cannot appreciate most modern art. Some of his work is stylized, but most of it is both realistic and exquisitely beautiful. His favorite subjects were portraits of theater greats and the black American, many of the latter being dancing figures.

If you watch many old black and white movies on late night television, you may have chanced to see a World War II film titled *Stage Door Canteen* about the Hollywood serviceman's club that was staffed by famous celebrities. The Stage Door Canteen did actually exist and was integrated more than most branches of the armed forces were at that time. The celebrity staff in the movie *Stage Door Canteen* was integrated by the inclusion of Richmond Barthe who worked as a dish washer in the kitchen, but was known to most cultured society of the day for his sculptural triumphs in Paris before returning to America at the outbreak of the war.

It wasn't until later that I learned two curious things; Barthe had been born the same year as my mother, and he had been born and raised in the same little town I had. Furthermore, Barthe was an Aquarius, as was I, and when I left he made me an Aquarius figure in bas-relief and signed it to me.

Barthe and I became fond of each other and would rap on everything from fine art to metaphysics to human relations. The trip up to his house, named Iolaus after a character in a Greek play, was through Fern Gully, a prehistoric riverbed filled with hundreds of varieties of ferns, some of which grow nowhere else in the world. It was a 'trip' in more ways than one, like entering another world both of environment and attitude.

Several things caused me to extend my trip longer than expected, not the least of which was the fact that I enjoyed my friendship with Barthe as well as the beauty of the island. Also, I needed further subsidy which I had hoped to get from Jamaican government sources and found slow in coming. Finally I learned that I had come to Jamaica less than a year before elections and it looked like no one was going to spend a nickel until afterward. I began to sneak piano gigs at the hotels, trying to hold on

170

by tooth and nail, but after a second six-month odyssey, I had to give up and return to the States.

I had taken two movie cameras, one an unsophisticated but rugged and reliable old spring-wound newsreel camera, the other a brand new reflex electric-drive model with all the bells and whistles. After the first few rolls from the new camera came back from the stateside processors okay, I stored the balance of exposed film in the refrigerator to eliminate the cost of shuttling it back and forth from the processors. This failed to reveal, however, that shortly thereafter the brand new camera developed shutter problems and only about a third of the footage I had shot was usable, and most of that was with the thirty year old newsreel camera. Fortunately, there was enough footage to combine with the hundreds of stills I shot from Barthe's files and the hours of recorded interviews I taped with him to make the film, if only I could find another $5,000 for post-production services.

I returned to the States to face not only a total lack of interest for a black educational series produced by a white film maker, but also to the most horrendous year I would experience up to that point in my life.

Chapter 12
THE AGE OF MARTYRS

The sixties was an age of martyrs; the Kennedys, Martin Luther King, the kids at Kent State, as well as people like Lord Buckley and Lenny Bruce, who were not shot with bullets, but who many feel were assassinated nonetheless.

I am not paranoid about my government, its military forces, or its police departments. I do not think they are a quasi-fascist group waiting for me to step out of the party line. I have been in fascist countries and known fascist individuals; countries that had beautiful scenery and individuals who loved good music and fine art, and I have seen how oppression can change the citizenry into pained, frustrated, silent robots in even the sunniest of climes. America is not like that, and it is not like that largely because it has had people like John Kennedy and Martin Luther King, and even Lord Buckley and Lenny Bruce to keep it from becoming like that. The irony is that men like these, who preached understanding instead of violence, were the targets of violence from the body politic that they respected and tried to refine.

Those who perpetrate such acts of violence with the rationalization that the end justifies the means, from the new regime I saw beheading thousands of Chinese in a flickering Moviola, to the individuals some believe induced Lord Buckley's 'heart attack' and Lenny Bruce's 'overdose,' I'm sure see themselves as the 'antibodies' in the body politic, protecting it from infection. In their shortsightedness they forget that antibodies are the same things that tolerate a cancer, defend its growth, and frustrate the surgeon's effort to excise the lethal tumor.

Who then is the villain, the surgeon with his invading knife or the antibody who defends the cancer? The cancer is, of course, the villain, but the antibody can't tell the difference between a cancer or a surgeon, and some surgeons are almost as confused at times. They both do a service at times, and at times they're both so fanatic in their singular missions they defeat their own ideologies with their shortsightedness and self righteousness.

Most artists are egocentric, probably Kennedy and King were too, but Kennedy, King, Buckley, and Bruce never played at omnipotence or presumed to snuff anyone for the good of the cause. Omnipotence was more the bag of Johnson and Nixon, Hitler and Stalin. It is also a little scary and a lot more insidious that many of the microcosms of the body politic, the little 'antibodies' just doing their job, from soldiers in Vietnam to vice officers in Los Angeles, are tempted to play God and do so more often than TV's idea of cops and robbers would have us believe.

The assassin's crime is beyond murder. It is not just the taking of a life, it is presuming to judge who shall die, a choice made not at random, but most often made on the basis of the victim's behavior, the victim's ideology, the victim's words and prayers and hopes for humanity. And the assassin's guilt is not his alone. It is shared to a very large degree by all who conspire to help him, and, ultimately, by all who ignore his crime after it is committed.

If an assassin, or any of those who share his guilt, is to find punishment in his lifetime, it is likely to be a result of his victim becoming a martyr. Martyrs have a habit of echoing across time, the very words and deeds that made them the assassin's target becoming legend to haunt the guilty. I find it curious that those who had the most to gain by Kennedy's and King's death, themselves had their careers tumble to ignoble depths and death a few short years after the assassinations.

All martyrs are not prophets and all prophets are not martyrs.

Marcus Garvey, who led a back-to-Africa movement during the early twenties, was a prophet whose principal issue failed, but whose prophecies rang true in the course of history, yet he died in relative comfort and obscurity not long after his firebrand career. The American housewife who immolated herself on the steps of the Los Angeles Federal Building to protest the Vietnamese War elected to be a martyr probably because life had not given her the prophet's gift or opportunity to otherwise express that most important truth she felt so passionate about.

There is a tendency, however, for the role of prophet or martyr to manifest each other. Many an obscure soul has become a martyr to a cause which, belatedly through family, friends, comrades, or historians, has sought to find the making of a prophet in the martyr's earlier life. More often, though, a person like Lenny who prophecies the awakening of a citizenry to the hypocrisies political, industrial, and religious leaders use to exploit that citizenry, having become a prophet, must anticipate becoming a martyr.

When I came back from Jamaica in 1965, a little more than a year before Lenny died, I found a man struggling with the realization that he was no longer headed toward the kinds of success he had hoped for in his life, that instead he was in the midst of an even greater challenge which he did not really want, but which he nonetheless accepted bravely and honestly.

Lenny was in the midst of his martyrdom. He could not get work, club owners had been warned, and shown through repeated arrests during Lenny's performances and other forms of harassment, that hiring Lenny was choosing sides in a revolutionary war against the establishment. Lenny could not go out of his house without being under surveillance, the embarrassment of repeated personal and vehicle searches, and bringing this cloud of paranoia and harassment to those with whom he came in contact.

Lenny was also ill. He had undergone major lung surgery for conditions which had been aggravated, if not caused, by drug abuse, and these considerable medical expenses were now added to his mounting legal expenses. Lenny was no longer sleek and tanned. Now he was bloated and ruddy, which may look healthy on a Scotsman, but read like a million miles of bad road on a Galician Jew.

His personal and creative energies were consumed by his legal defense against the establishment, or that small part of the establishment that felt threatened by him. The more they hounded him, the more that threat became more specific. Where Lenny began with a humorous but incisive analysis of the judicial system and the unappreciated cop on the beat who faces the hostility of social activism ("And the people are yelling Gestapo at every blue uniform. 'Gestapo, you schmuck, I'm the mail man'"), by 1965 he was bitterly recounting from the stage the disillusioning challenges to his faith in the system from arresting officers perjuring themselves with false testimony, to judges soliciting bribes from him.

At a time when his career should have been peaking, a time when he desperately needed the income, the few public appearances he could get were hampered by his health and his increasing obsession to stand on stage with volumes of court transcript and lecture on law to a dwindling audience who laughed at the wrong places, out of embarrassment, or not at all. At this point, Lenny Bruce's humor was not sick, rather, Lenny himself was. And while the indelible truth still rang in his performance, it was a frightening truth too sober to be called funny.

He welcomed me as warmly as ever, but his whole

demeanor and environment were somehow more subdued. He had swapped the terrycloth robe for a patient's white hospital gown and wore it day and night, for he almost never left the house. The handsome beard I had taught him to carefully shape every day was now a shapeless mass of overgrown stubble.

Where before I had required him to pay me 50% of salary for my various duties, a requirement designed primarily to discipline him not to burden me with irrelevant or busy work just to keep me by his side, now there were absolutely no funds, and I refused to take the cameras, typewriters, office copiers, and other personal belongings he offered me in lieu of payment. I worked totally on the speculation that his career would survive and we would share some kind of reward.

I took another bread-and-butter job to stay afloat, this time with Birns and Sawyer, a motion picture equipment firm dealing in sales, rentals, and manufacturing. I worked on their catalogs, in sales, and in the design of underwater lights. The sales were interesting because we not only sold to the biggies, as I had with Lloyd's and Bob Gamble's, but Birns and Sawyer advertised internationally and we sold to a lot of large and small companies throughout the world. Where before my self-education in cinema had taught me a lot about the aesthetics of foreign film production by being a devotee of 'art film' houses and researching the history of cinema, in my new job I learned firsthand from filmmakers in India, Indochina, Pakistan, and Peru the idiosyncrasies of their particular markets and technologies.

I took an apartment two blocks away on Vine Street next door to the music union building, in a huge old apartment house that looked like it came out of a Charles Addams cartoon. Out of my side window I could see the second floor of the union building, where years before business agents had sent me out to all kinds of unlikely piano gigs where the walls were lined with 8 x 10 glossies of athletes and the piano competed with shuffleboards and TV s over the bar blaring sports events. Out of my back window I could see the block I had lived on with Sandy and Chris which was soon to be a parking lot for Desilu Studios.

The apartment building was largely tenanted with what were then called hippies, just as my contemporaries when I was their age had been called beatniks, social nonconformists by any name. Many of these flower children were teenage girls and, as I was then slightly over thirty and seeing friends like Lenny age visibly before my eyes, I became acutely sensitive to the message in their nubile bodies. I realized that it wouldn't be too long before I myself would be entering middle age, and it suddenly dawned on me that I had never known an American teenage girl. When I was a teenager, I was busy seducing my high school teachers, and most of my flaming youth was spent learning it all from 'sophisticated older women' in their twenties and even older.

Now that I was 'even older' myself and finding a few gray hairs in my beard, I took another look at the girl next door named Lou, who seemed to play den mother to a whole parade of girls her age who passed in and out of her apartment. I didn't have to look twice before Lou invited herself over to play my grand piano. She sat beside me on the piano bench, and halfway through a childish rendition of *Chop Sticks*, she hesitated, looked at me sideways with a questioning expression, and said, "Do you wanna fuck?"

No woman before Lou had ever propositioned me so bluntly and with a four-letter word. I knew a lot of butch gals with garbage mouths, and the Cosmo Alley waitress and part-time sculptor's model who wanted me to throw Maxi out of the apartment said that four letter word in every other sentence, but never in its literal sense. Like an awful lot of women, she'd say it, she'd do it, but she wouldn't be caught dead saying she'd do it.

When I confessed that I could muster an interest, Lou peeled off her t-shirt and jeans, her only attire, and bounced on the bed in a kneeling position. As I stripped, she said, "Just one thing, I want you to enjoy me like a condemned man eating his last meal, 'cause I may not be here tomorrow."

She made me think of Mary Murray in Jamaica and, as I wondered if Mary was still living, I said, "Why, what's wrong?"

"Nothing," she smiled cheerily. "It's just that I believe romance should be enjoyed one day at a time. If I do see you again, I don't want you to think you own me just because you've fucked me, and if I never see you again, I'd rather remember you as a great fuck." That topped the Cosmo Alley waitress. two 'fucks' in one sentence.

Lou's philosophy may have been naive and oversimplified, but it seemed to work for her at that age. I let her make all the advances for a month until once, when I hadn't seen her for a week and extended an invitation she wasn't free to accept, she went in her apartment and pulled out a shy, but shapely little redhead who Lou blatantly announced would appreciate, enjoy, and adhere to Lou's philosophy. Lou kept me supplied for a long time. I would religiously check the girl's IDs to verify their legal age, get them jobs, ferry them to free clinics, supply Lou's apartment occasionally with food, and conduct birth control classes with on-the-job training.

Meanwhile, the job at Bims and Sawyer did bring about one minor change, they wanted me to shave off my beard. They thought of themselves as a very conservative firm. I figured, if I was going to part with it, I might as well make a production out of it. I suggested to Lenny we shoot a comedy sequence of his shaving me a la Laurel and

Hardy. He loved the idea, so I blew up and lathered some balloons and tried to teach him how to use a straight razor. After he popped half a box of balloons, I said there was no way I was going to let him shave me with a straight razor. He said he'd use a safety razor, but I felt it would lose any comic effect if I didn't have the straight razor to be afraid of. Besides, who ever saw a barber use a safety razor? Then Lenny decided that, if I was going to remove my beard, he would too, so we shot some stills of us shaving each other and a movie sequence of Lenny shaving his own beard off. It was a bit of silliness, but it was also a sort of symbolic gesture that we were now going to make some concession to the real world and get down to business.

Lenny wanted to write a book about his legal hassles, not just a crusade for free speech and the first amendment, but a case study of how the theory crumbles under the weight of an overburdened judicial system fat with the vested interests of lawyers and judges. He wanted to call it *The Law is a Vending Machine.*

He was almost daily in the courtroom battle scene, trying secretly to tape the courtroom dialogue on the equipment I had customized for him years before. Not all courts tape their proceedings or will sell you such tapes, which is an added expense if they do. Also, it has happened that the crucial tape or parts thereof are sometimes unavailable, and many times the written transcript does not always reflect the exact statements made, and certainly not those made off the record. Taping the proceedings yourself, which was illegal then, was the only way for you to have the same information the prosecutor had.

The first thing I did was repair and rebuild the concealed recorders Lenny used to tape court proceedings. The pocket-sized recorders were now obsolete, requiring constant transfer to larger reels to conform to the playback and filing system. They were replaced with an ever changing variety of smaller and smaller subminiature recorders. The major unit, an attache case containing a recorder whose 5" reels and super slow 15/16 ips speed allowed hours of continuous recording without reloading, had to be completely rebuilt.

In rebuilding it, Lenny asked if I could incorporate a still camera to shoot candids of some of the courtroom scenes to include in the book. There were 35mrn cameras available with auto exposure and motor drive that would fit that need, but Lenny had never mastered loading a 35mrn camera and they were fairly expensive. There were also cheap auto exposure, motor-driven, Instamatic cartridge loading cameras, but there were no fast lenses or films available for them to deal with the available light in courtroom situations.

I showed Lenny the 16-mm movie camera I had built into a transistor radio and used in my investigative work, explaining that the camera could shoot still frames as well as movies, and the stills from it wouldn't be any worse than those we blew up for the presentation album of *The Leather Jacket.* Lenny was enthralled with the idea of a concealed movie camera and revised the whole project to become a documentary film with the same title and theme.

I built the movie camera into the attache case with the recorder, and I also concealed one in a law book. Despite the simplicity of the system, which was as easy to load as a cartridge razor and designed to require no exposure or focus settings, Lenny didn't have the coordination of manual dexterity and visual timing to use it effectively. I have over 1,000 feet of color movies Lenny shot with those cameras which are totally incomprehensible blurs and swishes. Eventually, I had to go to the courtrooms myself to utilize the concealed movie cameras.

In logical preparation for a backer's presentation,

and primarily to lift Lenny's sagging spirits, I designed, shot, and edited some titles for the film. There was a beautifully proportioned meter maid in Hollywood who I wanted to film for the opening. My titles opened with a very tight shot of her derriere, the bold title *The Law* appearing above it simultaneously with the heavy opening chords of Liszt's *Hungarian Rhapsody No.2*. As she bouncily pulls away from the camera, we discover the object of our adoration belongs to a meter maid who stops beside a car parked at a meter, dismounting with her citation book while the camera pans and zooms into a closeup of the meter which just then flips to "Violation." The balance of the title, *Is A Vending Machine*, wipes on in script beneath *The Law* as the music segues abruptly to the frolicking third movement of the *Hungarian Rhapsody*.

I tried in vain for weeks to surreptitiously get the footage of my title's leading lady to coincide with a meter flipping to violation. Finally, I found a meter which would flip to violation if I tapped it, and attached a radio-operated solenoid to its hidden side. I parked my car at the expired meter in front of it, and concealed my camera across and down the street at an angle which, when she dismounted to cite my car, would allow me to pan to the rigged meter which I then flipped to violation via the radio-controlled solenoid. It cost me film, lab, opticals (superimposition of titles), a parking ticket, and also the solenoid with its radio receiver which she discovered and confiscated when she cited the poor soul whose car was parked behind mine.

But it delighted Lenny, making him more enthused about the project and more animated than I had seen him in years. It also reminded him that I was the artist who had contributed much of the cinematographic elements of his earlier works. He had come to think of me as a technician, my hands so frequently occupied with jeweler's screwdrivers and soldering guns, the man who tried to make a physical reality of his nebulous dreams.

Even when I worked at Cosmo Alley, Lenny never heard me play the piano nor knew I wrote words and music; after all, I was not a hip junkie jazz musician . Even when my creations were published in other media, he did not want to know about it, after all, it was not in Hollywood or in the Hollywood image.

That thirty seconds of titles caused Lenny to reflect on all I had done over the years for him more than any single thing. He asked to see some of my industrial films, such fifteen and thirty minute epics as *Communications in the Community,* a black community PR film for the Southern California Gas Company, and *Paradise Found,* a Jamaican travel promotion film. He was impressed with the films and particularly my visual openings, like the time lapse fade-in of a sunrise over the Los Angeles skyline as seen from Mulholland Drive, followed by a 360 degree pan of the city seen from the newly constructed Water Department building. He loved the Jamaican film opening with a montage of water scenes, river rafting, Dunn's River Falls, a cloudburst in Fern Gully, and water inundating my camera in its underwater housing, the water receding to reveal each new shot.

Lenny was now quieter, more serious. Economics had probably forced him to dry out from drugs for longer periods. His words of praise were less flamboyant, but more sincere, and they occurred more frequently and more believably, not just when it was time to pay the bill or when there was a strategic audience.

Lenny looked at my films, then blinked and said, "Wow, man, I knew you were talented, but I never dreamed. No wonder you were hacked with me when we made *The Leather Jacket,* but don't worry, we'll finish it and a lot more." Then he looked a little apprehensive and added, "You will help me finish *The Leather Jacket,* won't you?"

I flipped the rewind on the projector and replied,

"You were the first to put a movie camera in my hands so I could be the first to film *The Leather Jacket*. Why shouldn't I finish it?"

But the film that consumed our efforts then was *The Law is a Vending Machine,* and as the material for it piled up, Lenny saw the opportunity of a pre-film spinoff which might provide some sorely needed income. He had recently done some prison time for one of his drug busts, despite the fact that he was always vindicated in higher courts for the obscenity cases. He used to wear his denim prison uniform like a badge of honor, sometimes on stage. He used this prison release to title his last comedy album, *Lenny Bruce Is Out Again,* based on the preliminary material for the film. He shaped the material better than he had in recent times when his stage presence had deteriorated, and he performed it in some of the last live appearances he made on stage. While that last album is almost entirely about law and more somber than funny in spots, it was the most incisive statement of what those last years of his life were about.

The night we shot the album cover, Lenny had not really pinned down how he wanted to pictorialize it. My suggestions were, as usual, too ambitious for the budget or schedule. I saw composite photography or artwork of him in prison uniform eluding bloodhounds, prison guards in a tower machine gun nest, or Frankie done up as a shotgun- toting southern sheriff. The lack of time or daylight precluded my location shot suggestions, such as Lenny coming out of a hole in the ground with the prison in the background, Lenny floating down a rat-infested underground sewer in a rubber raft, or Lenny emerging free from the prison gates to be greeted by a bevy of beauties and Frankie as a flasher.

We futzed around, shooting indoor color pictures of Lenny chained to the black rock wall of John Judnich's bedroom, reading from a variety of books held one at a time in each picture: *The Bible, Nietzsche, Mein Kampf, The Communist Manifesto, Popular Mechanics.* We busted our brains trying to relate props around the house to the album title until about sunrise when I ran out of film for my camera. We had an impossible deadline to meet and, at the last minute, Lenny pulled out a cheap twin-lens reflex he owned, loaded with black-and- white film. As the sun tried to peep through the morning smog, we went out into the garden of the triangular hillside lot toward the comer Lenny considered his hideaway where he would escape from hangers-on who sometimes overpopulated the house. In the garden was an object Lenny considered a satire of typical garden sculpture, a damaged four foot Victorian female figure standing in the bowl of a broken toilet, the tank of which was used as a planter. Lenny composed variations of himself seated, fully clothed, behind the toilet bowl so that he appeared to be sitting on the john reading a newspaper while the statue peered over his shoulder. Though it didn't relate to the album title or material, I sensed that Lenny felt toilets had a deep rooted significance in his life. With the cheap little camera I photographed the man I had found in a 'toilet,' the man whose last album cover would include a toilet, and the man who would die in a toilet.

The hectic deadline for the album cover was because I had to process, print, and set typography for a cover mockup before that afternoon when Lenny had a now rare guest shot on *The Steve Allen Show.* Of all the famous who lauded Lenny, the one who was there first and last, and was most loyal was Steve Allen.

The back of that last album cover lists twenty-one lawyers, some of whom may have drained his last coins, but most of whom sincerely believed in his cause and donated their services. Also on the back of that album cover is a letter from one supporter who discovered Lenny very late in his career, but who had a wider chasm to cross than most. The Reverend Sidney Lanier of St. Clement's Church in New York City stated the following:

"I was curious to see if you were really as penetrating a critic of our common hypocrisies as I had heard. I found that you are an honest man, sometimes a shockingly honest man, and I wrote you a note to say so. It is never popular to be so scathingly honest, whether it is from a nightclub stage or from a pulpit. ... I emphatically do *not* believe your act is obscene in intent. The method you use has a lot in common with most serious critics (the prophet or the artist, not the professor) of society .... Clearly your intent is not to excite sexual feelings or to demean, but to shock us awake to the realities of racial hatred and invested absurdities about sex and birth and death, to move toward sanity and compassion. It is clear that you are intensely angry at our hypocrisies, yours as well as mine, and at the highly subsidized mealy-mouthism that passes as wisdom."

Reverend Lanier's voice was a most singular one from the clergy who, with a few exceptions, violently condemned Lenny or remained ominously silent about this man who addressed their profession and was taken to court on charges which amounted to 'blasphemy.' His gesture was immensely generous and merciful to a man who was so totally rejected by the society he so desperately wanted to be part of and to serve with his talents.

The little fortress up on the hill began to be like a prison where a man physically ill and economically deprived finally became emotionally depressed. Lenny rarely ever talked about death. Once on stage, he reminisced about departed comedy stars and said, "I'd like to go about 43, I guess. This may sound psychotic to you, but I never thought of killing myself, never, but if I did, I'd want to be unique. Headlines, 'Sick comic succumbs, swallows 650 dexamine spangiels. He was killed by his neighbors for talking too much.'"

Alone on the hill with John and me he would sit daily with the tape recorders, throw the little switch on the mike, and begin with the preamble I heard over and over, "So they had the trial, so I get found guilty and it's ten months later and I've been in this room and in other rooms, er, spending about ten hours a day, er, talking to myself, er, trying to figure out a way to vindicate myself because if the judge would've seen me work he wouldn't have busted me."

The last few months, though, the depression bottomed out. I realized why later, when I discovered among those garbage tapes some very private conversations with Honey. Around that time there was an epidemic of overdose cases, seven in seven days, a total of nineteen in thirty days, all on the rarity of pure heroin, all in the same general geographic and professional area, all people known to Lenny. Honey received the 'gift' of three spoons of pure heroin, an unheard of boon, from a total stranger. As she was telling Lenny, she discovered he was secretly recording her and he said, "If I don't tape it, no one will believe it."

At the time, Lenny was completely rational and convinced he was not unduly paranoid, as he described to Honey his concern that the dangerously pure heroin floating around was intended for him. He described the audacity of risking human lives in order to tempt him as a 'religious test,' as opposed to a 'legal test.'

Whether or not Lenny had become resigned to such a fate, there was an unusual calm about him those last few weeks. He was less uptight about the schedule and progress of my editing the documentary. He'd let me take anything I wanted out of the film vault at Bekins: films, tapes, transcripts. Ten days before he died I had almost everything from the vault in my apartment, but I conscientiously returned practically all of it. Later, when I wanted to do a documentary about him, all those

187

materials, including the stills and movies I had never been paid for from the beginning, were in the hands of another whose documentary, *Lenny Bruce Without Tears,* I felt did not do Lenny justice.

I had heard from a customer at Birns and Sawyer that *The Happy Wanderers* television travel series was hiring cinematographers and my wanderlust led me to call them, which resulted in a request to see some of my work.

At about 10 P.M. Wednesday, August 3, 1966, I went up to Lenny's to get him to sign a note authorizing me to take some of the films I'd shot out of storage as that was the easiest sample footage I could get hold of to show the producers of *The Happy Wanderers.* Although he was still somewhat thicker and ruddier than in previous years, Lenny looked unusually well, happy, and calm. I know for a fact he was not high at that moment. He told me to forge a note for Bekins, to take anything I wanted out of there anytime I wanted, adding, "After all, Billums, it's yours as well as mine. Most of what's in there you helped make happen." The 'Billums' was Lenny's form of sincere affection, as much as such terms bridled me, but the creative acknowledgment was very unusual. It prompted me to ask about his welfare, and he said Sally had just come through that day with some bread for him. Just then Sally called, and he was very affectionate on the phone in his thank-you's to her, relaying greetings between Sally and me before he hung up.

Then he took me aside conspiratorially and told me, with childish glee illuminating his face, that the beautiful young girl who had been with him for several days and was at that moment cooking for him in the kitchen was the daughter of a judge. The implications of her presence haunted me for years after until I ultimately decided that those aspects of his death were not the most important issues of his life.

I squeezed his hand, smiled back at him, and tried

to mimic Sally, the eternal Jewish mother, as I said, "Enjoy, enjoy."

The head of a PR firm called me the next day on business, casually mentioning the 'tragedy' of Lenny's demise. I excused myself from the phone, then from the store, bought a paper to verify the story, and, with the feeling that I was running for my life, went straight to Bekins where they refused to release the materials I had intended to pick up that day. I called Sally and she said she had tried to get them without any success either.

At first I felt betrayed by Lenny. I had put all my eggs in his basket, given him my time, my talent, my faith, and my love, and he had pissed it all away for just another 'taste.' I could not participate in all the lamentations, the eulogies, the circuses. God, how the real people must have felt there elbow to elbow with all the pretenders, parasites, and publicity seekers.

I was born in '33, had always had a premonition that I would 'make it' when I was 33, and envisioned Lenny as the Christ who was crucified when he was 33. Instead, when I was 33 Lenny died and shortly thereafter my mother died.

I wanted to do a documentary about Lenny and, when that was thwarted, I considered doing a book. I first conceived it as a scholarly study of comedy, the distinctive styles and contributions of the comedians I had known and worked with, principally Lenny and the importance of his life and work. I was, however, discouraged by the rash of articles and material by people who had never known Lenny, works that smacked of idolatry or came off like an autopsy of a junkie, and I did not want to become a vulture contesting the spoils with the other vultures.

The polarity of public feeling about Lenny continued to haunt me.

I had long ago faced the conservatives who, with one stroke of prejudice against 'junkies,' 'Jews, 'blasphemers,' or 'blue comedians,' swept away the insight Lenny's words offered about our times. But I became increasingly aware of the growing number of young liberals yearning to be 'hip' who interpreted these second-hand caricatures of Lenny as an endorsement of the drug culture.

To those young liberals I wanted desperately to say that all the positive things in Lenny and his work were in no way derived from drugs. They were derived from the talent and genius inherent in Lenny from childhood before he ever heard of drugs, and the opportunity for those positive things to reach an audience was largely derived from the efforts of three 'straights' like Sally, Frankie, and me. Don't tell me I don't know what drugs do or don't contribute to creativity because I haven't 'shot up' myself. I have habitated and hassled with those who shot up on three different continents, seen many beautiful and talented people seek the easy way to truth and happiness through the tiny tunnel of a needle, and never once saw an ounce of it as an asset to creativity, but a hell of a lot of liability to health, happiness, and everything they sought.

This is not preaching; it is imploring you to not look for perfection in your models, to accept the responsibility to analyze and discern what is valid from the invalid in them, and to appreciate and enjoy what is good without mistakenly swallowing whole what is bad. There is so much to love and learn from Lenny that there is no need for anyone to champion his faults.

To the conservatives I can only say the same things, and add that when you persist in looking for perfect models you will only find them in the past, a past that manipulators and exploiters, hecklers and historians, will always manage to mold to whatever image you are seeking, rounding off the imperfections you cannot tolerate here and now. But the here and now is where you and I live, and the future is what you and I and those who have shared our lifetime make it; the Kennedys, the Kings, the Lord Buckleys, and the Lenny Bruces.

In this mortal realm there is no perfection, but there is hope. If we are to build a brave new world, a heaven on earth, then we must do so from these imperfect parts of the here and now. If we can sift gold from dirt and distill wine from rotting fruit, then why can't we discern rare wisdom from a man of a different color or culture? If we cannot, then we will surely crucify the next messiah and all the prophets that precede him.

I recognize Lenny Bruce as a man who was imperfect in many ways, but a martyr and a prophet nonetheless. It is not prior intent nor the sacrifice of life that assigns these labels. Rather, it is the thrust of one's life and its ultimate impact on society which determines that such as Lenny be so remembered in history. We must strive to be open to all viewpoints, to perceive and appreciate the prophetic message we are constantly offered from a myriad of unlikely sources, and to recognize Lenny Bruce as such an unlikely source.

Few suffered more from his imperfections than I, but if I can forgive his faults, then those who never suffered them must surely forgive him. If I can define a philosopher as one who understands they are not bound to other's conceptions of reality as long as they are willing to rationally perceive their own reality, then I can define a prophet as one who not only perceives a better reality, but can also communicate it.

Sitting on the flying bridge of that Chris Craft in Jamaica back in 1960, I wrote a brief verse that tried to express this concept:

> Each man is his own God,
> His petty ego
>> which cannot save him from
>> a falling boulder or a thunderbolt,

Is nonetheless what drives him
     to carve the boulder into block
     and contain the thunderbolt
     in a glass bottle,
And in proportion to his faith in himself
He will serve as his own divinity.

Whether or not God created man, it is man who has evolved himself through the mechanical age and the electronic age. Whether or not God shall judge man, it is man who must make himself Godlike, who must see his own flaws without rancor and evolve and refine his civilization and society without the compulsion of denial which makes him resent and persecute those such as Lenny Bruce who affect this process.

If I needed a whole book to say these things, it's because I had to reveal myself and my cohorts, Sally and Frankie, to you, for we were part of the making of a prophet. I had to qualify us as humans; imperfect, but talented, perceptive, and with a capacity to love and persevere with Lenny without the motive of money or drugs and with the faith that humanity would ultimately recognize his work.

If you find anything of value in my words, then I hope and pray you will believe me when I say, we live in a world of many philosophers and very few prophets, and if we fail to learn how they come to be and what they can teach us, we may become dumb bystanders at their crucifixion.

THE END

PHOTO GALLERY

Upper Left: Frank Ray Perelli, c. 1952.
Upper right: Frankie, c. 1955, as star of "Legends of Pancho Villa," a TV western series in which the legendary hero is a Mexican Robin Hood; Disney never produced this epic, which remained a pilot. *Left:* William Karl Thomas, c. 1952.

The first professional studio portrait of Lenny Bruce, shot by Karl Thomas in 1957. It began a decade of putative 50–50 collaboration between the two men.

Lenny with the author's .380 MAB pistol *(left)* and Pancho Villa's dagger *(below)*. The pictures are from Karl Thomas's first character photo layout of Lenny Bruce, 1957.

Lenny on a picnic. One of the twelve photos shot by author for Lenny Bruce's first album cover, after the idea of Lenny cooking hot dogs between his fingers while getting zapped in an electric chair was rejected because the props cost too much.

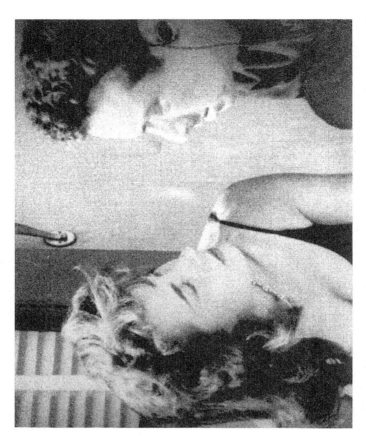

Blowup of a frame from the first day's filming of *The Leather Jacket*. This pilot sequence shows Jean Hidey and Lenny in the first encounter of the principle characters.

Lenny in the third scene of *The Leather Jacket*, immediately before filming was interrupted by a real-life clergyman in full regalia, who accused Bruce and Karl Thomas (behind the camera) of being "Jews."

Left to right: Bill Himes, Frankie Ray, Lenny Bruce, Karl Thomas. Himes voices one of many aesthetic differences with the author, while Lenny painfully tries to arbitrate.

Pet Cemetery. Various scenes and sight gags for *The Leather Jacket* were shot here. Curiously, and no doubt coincidentally, a number of virtually identical scenes are found in *The Loved One*, a later Hollywood film based on the Evelyn Waugh novel of that name.

Mother and daughter: Sally *(left)* and Kitty, age three, photographed by the author.

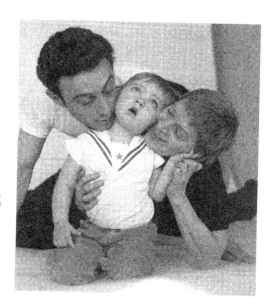

The family at home, though Kitty's eyes are seeing higher things. Photo by Karl Thomas.

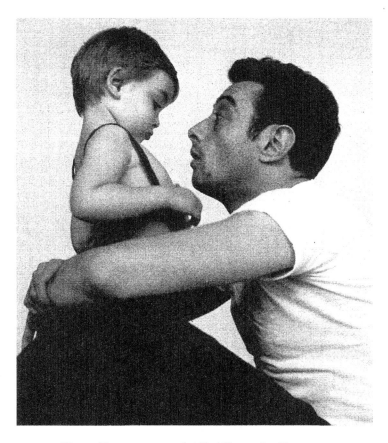

Kitty and Lenny, unaware that Karl Thomas has his camera.

Above: Karl Thomas with the 35mm Mitchell NC camera used for feature and location filmings in Mexico, Arizona, and California. *Left:* Thomas with Lloyd Berman's old 35mm Arriflex, trashed by a union goon during filming of *The Leather Jacket.*

204

Above: Karl Thomas on a research trip in Port Antonio, Jamaica; the hotel Chris Craft is seen in the background. *Right:* Richmond Barthe in his Ocho Rios studio during filming of the author's unfinished series on Afro-American education.

205

One of many rejected concepts for the cover of "Lenny Bruce Is Out Again," the last album. The wall is actually in Lenny's Hollywood Hills home. Photo by author.

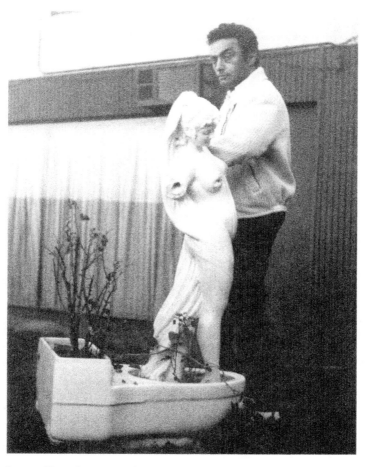

Lenny with garden statue and unconventional planter, from the final layout for the last album. Photo by Karl Thomas.

The final album cover. It was prepared just hours before airtime so Lenny could solicit mail order sales during an appearance on the Steve Allen show. Later, Phil Spector distributed this album with the same photo but slicker typography. Collectors prize the few rare disks without the "Phille" label, and with this crude cover. Photo by author.

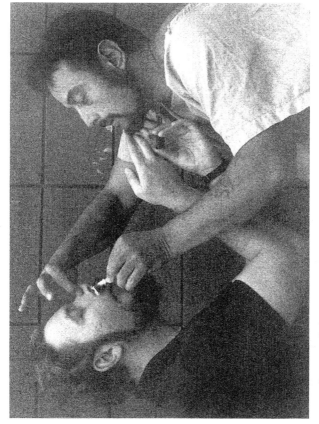

Lenny and the author shave each other as a "conformist" gesture during filming of *The Law Is a Vending Machine,* only months before Lenny died.

OTHER BOOKS BY
WILLIAM KARL THOMAS

All books are available in print and digital editions from Amazon.com. Find details and excerpts of all books, or order autographed copies at Media Maestro - Book Division, P.O. Box 50672, Tucson, AZ 85703, or online at www.mediamaestro.net/books.htm

 ## LENNY BRUCE: THE MAKING OF A PROPHET
The book you have just read is available in hardcover or an E-edition for your Kindle, Nook, I-pad, or other E-reader, or read it on your computer by downloading Amazon's free E-reader application. Tell your friends they can get the E-edition instantly online for less than the postage it would cost to mail your print copy across the nation.
ISBN #978-0-9799477-0-4 Hardcover: $24.95
ISBN #978-1-62768-003-5 Softcover $9.95
ISBN #978-0-9799477-4-2 Digital E-edition $4.99

 ## THE CANDY BUTCHER
The amazing biography of screenwriter, film producer, playwrite, actor, nightclub comedian Frank Ray Perilli, creator of such notable films as *The Doberman Gang, Harlow* and such cult films as *Dracula's Dog, Little Cigars, Fairytales, Cinderella, The End of the World, Alligator,* and more than two dozen unique offbeat films and plays.
ISBN #978-1-62768-019-6 Softcover $9.95
ISBN: 978-1-62768-020-2 digital E-edition $2.99

THE PIANO LOVER a trilogy

In New Orleans French Quarter during the 1950's, a young male cocktail pianist's life is complicated by four beautiful women: two young women from opposite poles of society who love him in diverse ways, and two middle aged women who seek to control him for their own secret reasons.

ISBN #978-1-62768-005-9 Softcover $14.95
ISBN: 978-1-62768-006-6 digital E-edition $4.99

PIANO LOVER THE MUSICAL

The second novel of *The Piano Lover* trilogy includes the script and score of an entire original musical stage production. Follow the careers of the talented alumni from New Orleans French Quarter who helped create the 1950's and 1960's counter culture.

ISBN #978-1-62768-011-0 Softcover $14.95
ISBN: 978-1-62768-012-7 digital E-edition $4.99

PIANO LOVER THE MOVIE

In the third novel of the trilogy, the musical is made into a movie. The entourage experience professional and romantic adventures in Hollywood, San Francisco, and exotic foreign capitals with their famous and celebrated show biz peers.

ISBN #978-1-62768-013-4 Softcover $14.95
ISBN: 978-1-62768-014-1 digital E-edition $4.99

MORE BOOKS ON NEXT PAGE

CLEO

A novel about a beautiful and talented black female journalist who is an intimate friend of black entertainment and political celebrities during the turbulent civil rights era in the 1950's and 1960's. Her professional and private life takes a quantum leap when she crosses paths with a cynical but equally talented white male publicist.

ISBN: 978-1-62768-002-8 Softcover $9.95
ISBN: 978-0-9799477-6-6 digital E-edition $2.99

THE JOSAN AND THE JEE

A novel about three women who survived massacres and rape during The Korean War, and their intimate relationship with an American GI dealing with his own demons from his failed marriage to his unfaithful stateside wife to his contentious relationship with his bigoted military boss.

ISBN: 978-1-62768-001-1 Softcover $9.95
ISBN: 978-0-9799477-5-9 digital E-edition $2.99

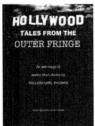

HOLLYWOOD TALES FROM THE OUTER FRINGE

William Karl Thomas' career brought him in contact with 'A' list celebrities and the armies of 'little people' who served them. This anthology of twelve short stories reveals the intimate relationship between the two set against a historically accurate 1950's-1960's background.

ISBN: 978-0-9799477-3-5 Softcover: $9.95
ISBN: 978-0-9799477-7-3 digital E-edition $2.99

THE GENTEEL POOR

A memoir telling the story of four generations of the author's colorful and talented family spanning the Civil War, World War I, the Great Depression, and World War II. This coming of age memoir deals with the social and ethnic evolution of the New Orleans/Gulf Coast area a century before it was devastated by Hurricane Katrina.

ISBN: 978-1-59663-565-4 Hardcover: $29.95
ISBN: 978-1-62768-000-4 Softcover $9.95
ISBN: 978-0-9799477-9-7 digital E-edition $2.99

A PLACE FOR US

The biography of Wendy Wolf who entered an iron lung at the age of four and emerged a polio survivor whose life illustrates the challenges of opportunity and acceptance people with disabilities face and the triumphs and successes this extraordinary woman achieved.

ISBN: 978-0-9799477-2-8 Hardcover $29.95
ISBN: 978-1-62768-004-2 Softcover $9.95
ISBN: 978-0-9799477-8-0 digital E-edition $2.99

MORE BOOKS ON NEXT PAGE

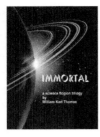

IMMORTAL: a science fiction trilogy

A millennium into the future, three alien archeologists attempt to determine how humanity self destructed themselves and their planet. Their discovery of a dormant android guarding a human gene bank on a Saturnian moon leads to a conflict among them regarding humanity's potential future. Share the alien archeologist's discovery of human evolution and the turning points that shaped earth's civilizations in the first book of this trilogy.

ISBN: 978-1-62768-007-3 Softcover $9.95
ISBN: 978-1-62768-008-0 digital E-edition $2.99

IMMORTAL: RESURRECTION (early 2016)

In the second novel of the trilogy, the alien female allies with the android's desperate attempt to resurrect humanity while alien forces mount an expedition to rid the universe of human dysfunctional behavior.

ISBN: 978-1-62768-015-8 Softcover $9.95
ISBN: 978-1-62768-016-5 digital E-edition $2.99

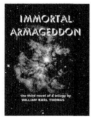

IMMORTAL: ARMAGEDDON (late 2016)

In the third novel of the trilogy, a small band of newly created humans defend the survival of the human race against an alien expedition determined to rid the universe of future human folly, and the origin and mission of the android is revealed.

ISBN: 978-1-62768-017-2 Softcover $9.95
ISBN: 978-1-62768-018-9 digital E-edition $2.99

ABOUT THE AUTHOR

 William Karl Thomas was born 1/25/33 in Bay St. Louis, Mississippi, a small Gulf Coast town in which Tennessee Williams lived and wrote about in his works. In 1951 Thomas married his former high school teacher and was divorced after a four year childless marriage. His checkered background includes being a cocktail pianist in New Orleans French Quarter, serving a year of combat in the Air Force during the Korean War, being a photographer, a journalist, a feature/documentary cinematographer, a screen writer, an industrial film producer, a public relations executive, and a book author. He has worked for and with such notables as Frank Sinatra, the Rat Pack, Lenny Bruce, Shecky Greene, and others.. In the course of various assignments, Thomas has lived or worked in Oxford England, Paris France, Japan, Korea, Jamaica, Mexico, Canada, and various parts of the United States.

In reviewing *Lenny Bruce: The Making of a Prophet,* The Manchester Guardian has stated, "Thomas can write. He superbly evokes the seedy atmosphere of the cheap Hollywood clubs and coffeehouses," and "His work sometimes reads like a Bogart script." An Amazon.com reader review states, "If you're interested in the inner workings of creative minds, then I highly recommend this book." Thomas' other works, including his fiction, are thoroughly researched and historically correct, as Kirkus notes in reviewing *The Josan and the Jee,* praising "...his historically astute depiction of the country and era."

.

Printed in Great Britain
by Amazon

77221908R00132